S. Hrg. 113–263

IMPORTING ENERGY, EXPORTING JOBS

HEARING

BEFORE THE

COMMITTEE ON
ENERGY AND NATURAL RESOURCES
UNITED STATES SENATE

ONE HUNDRED THIRTEENTH CONGRESS

SECOND SESSION

ON

"IMPORTING ENERGY, EXPORTING JOBS. CAN IT BE REVERSED?"

MARCH 25, 2014

Printed for the use of the
Committee on Energy and Natural Resources

U.S. GOVERNMENT PRINTING OFFICE

87–803 PDF   WASHINGTON : 2014

For sale by the Superintendent of Documents, U.S. Government Printing Office
Internet: bookstore.gpo.gov   Phone: toll free (866) 512–1800; DC area (202) 512–1800
Fax: (202) 512–2104   Mail: Stop IDCC, Washington, DC 20402–0001

CONTENTS

STATEMENTS

APPENDIXES

APPENDIX I

APPENDIX II

IMPORTING ENERGY, EXPORTING JOBS

TUESDAY, MARCH 25, 2014

U.S. SENATE,
COMMITTEE ON ENERGY AND NATURAL RESOURCES,
Washington, DC.

The committee met, pursuant to notice, at 10:06 a.m. in room SD–366, Dirksen Senate Office Building, Hon. Mary Landrieu, chair, presiding.

OPENING STATEMENT OF HON. MARY LANDRIEU, U.S. SENATOR FROM LOUISIANA

The CHAIR. Good morning, everyone. Thank the members for attending and thank our witnesses for being a part of this important hearing.

It's my pleasure to bring the Energy Committee to an opening session this morning on the subject of natural gas. Our title, "Importing Energy, Exporting Jobs. Can this be reversed?"

I just want to say to begin with that Senator Murkowski is on her way. She's in a very important meeting. We expect her momentarily and looking forward to her opening statement.

I want to thank Senator Ron Wyden, my dear friend and former leader of this committee, for his leadership and his support, former chairman of this committee. Look forward to continuing to working with him and all members of the committee on both sides of the aisle.

Not quite a decade ago members of this committee attended numerous meetings in this room to consider the 2005 Energy Policy Act. At that time we discussed, at length, the need to import more liquefied natural gas to meet our growing energy demands. Thanks to an extraordinarily and swift, extraordinary and swift advances in technology to locate, capture and produce natural gas, today this committee will discuss the expanded opportunities to export liquefied natural gas and the possibilities to create high paying jobs in America and support our allies in Europe and budding democracies across the world.

When President George W. Bush signed EPACT in 2005, the price of natural gas was averaging $9.50 cents per cubic feet. By October of that year, the price had risen to $13 and continued to rise in December of that year to $15. These high prices force chemical manufacturers to close up their factories and head overseas.

This affected many States, not just Louisiana, Michigan and other industrial States around the country. They did so in droves. The fact that less than 10 years later we are now in a 4-year period

(1)

of domestic gas prices at $5 or less is stunning, with only a long term favorable outlook ahead of us.

Because of this price reduction and price stabilization Methanex, for instance, the world's largest producer of methanol is literally breaking down a factory piece by piece in Chile and shipping it back to Geismar, Louisiana, where it originally was.

What caused this reversal of fortune?

What game changing technologies were involved?

What actions should this committee and the U.S. take given this new set of data and facts?

New discoveries in oil and gas have fortified our economy in the last few years buffering us from an even deeper recession which, I believe, would have occurred and providing new, high paying jobs for thousands of Americans. Nowhere is this more evident than in my home State of Louisiana and all along the Gulf Coast, America's energy coast. According to 2013, a study by David Dismukes at LSU, over 200,000 jobs will be created by new, unconventional production in Louisiana alone by 2019. This is not considering the other jobs in other States around the country. It is quite promising.

The oil and gas industry currently supports over 300,000 jobs in Louisiana and has been a major factor in securing below average unemployment for the last 5 years. For also for States such as North Dakota that have had increased ongoing production, Colorado, etcetera.

A recent LSU report estimated that from 2012 to 2018 approximately $47,000,000 of private sector investment will be made in new and existing plants and projects in Allen Parish, Beauregard, Calcasieu, Cameron and Jefferson Davis. Parishes that people on this committee have probably never heard of and people in America have never heard of either. But these are real places, with real people, 100-mile stretch between I-10 Lafayette and Lake Charles, Louisiana. That investment is expected to create more than 37,000 new jobs, high paying jobs.

In America LNG exports will not only drive continued investment in domestic production and create jobs they're also a powerful geo-political tool, particularly in light of Russia's illegal aggression in the Ukraine. The events in the Ukraine have shown that Russia President Putin is intent on using his monopoly on energy supplies to pressure our allies in Europe to advance his economic and philosophical agenda.

Last week Russia sanctioned 9 officials. I was one of them. Being sanctioned by President Putin is a badge of honor for me and the people that I represent.

It has only encouraged me to redouble my efforts to increase domestic energy production here in the United States and make the U.S. a global leader in energy exports. America can and should be an energy super power in all aspects of conventional and advanced sources of energy including new alternative fuels and alternative energy sources. We all know that real competition in real open markets drives efficiency and lowers prices for everyone.

The last thing Putin and his cronies want is competition from the United States of America in the energy race. Tyrants and dictators throughout history have had many reasons to fear revolutions. This U.S. energy revolution is one they should all keep their eyes on.

I look forward to playing a role to bring energy security independence to America and its democratic allies around the world to advance freedom of speech, freedom of religion and yes, the freedom of the press and to hold the new promise to hold leaders accountable for what they do. Today's hearing is part of this effort. Far too often when faced with complex and difficult challenges we stand still, unsure, hesitant, moving in every different direction. I can assure you this will not be the case with this committee under my leadership.

We will do our part to use our domestic production of gas, oil, advanced coal technologies, alternative fuel technologies and exciting renewables to meet our energy needs here at home and abroad. We will also break the stranglehold of tyrants and oppressors who use their energy stockpiles to crush the hopes and promise of freedom and democracy for all people, particularly women and girls.

We have a great panel of experts assembled here today. I look forward to hearing from them about how we can achieve these goals.

I will turn to Ranking Member Murkowski as soon as she's here for her opening statement. Until then, let me call on my—our witnesses this morning.

I do want to mention, for the record, and give credit to Senator Mark Udall, who is here with us this morning, on a bill that he has introduced that is currently pending. Hopefully we can take this up at some point, the American Job Creation and Strategic Alliances Act, cosponsored by Senator Begich. It amends a section of the Natural Gas Act to allow for exports of natural gas to world trade organization countries. We'll look forward to hearing more specifically about many other pieces of legislation on this subject, both pro and con and neutral, as we develop our policy. But I want to thank you, Senator Udall, for your introduction of this bill.

I'd like to put into the record an Op Ed that I thought was particularly on point from the Wall Street Journal, their editorial, a Gas Export Strategy and from the New York Times, from Thomas Friedman, From Putin, a Blessing in Disguise, for the record.

The CHAIR. Now I'd like to begin with our witnesses then we will go through a round of questions.

Our first is Mr. Adam Sieminski, Administrator of U.S. Information.

Next, Mr. David Montgomery, Senior Vice President of NERA Economic Consulting.

Next, Mr. Edward C. Chow, Senior Fellow, Energy and National Security Program Center for Strategic International Studies.

We're very pleased to have the Minister of Energy from the Republic of Lithuania that I think will give us a really extraordinary and very timely view of what's happening in his part of the world.

Then Mr. David Goldwyn, Nonresident Senior Fellow, Energy Security Initiative at Brookings Institute.

So please, Mr. Sieminski, if you could proceed with 5 minutes of testimony and then a round of questions.

Thank you.

STATEMENT OF ADAM SIEMINSKI, ADMINISTRATOR, ENERGY INFORMATION ADMINISTRATION, DEPARTMENT OF ENERGY

Mr. SIEMINSKI. Chair Landrieu, members of the committee, thank you very much for the opportunity to be here today. EIA, as you know, is the statistical and analytical agency.

The CHAIR. Could you speak a little bit closer into your microphone? All of you are going to have to press your buttons and then lean into the microphone. Thank you.

Mr. SIEMINSKI. Chair Landrieu, as you know, the EIA is the statistical and analytical agency within the Department of Energy. By law its data and analyses are independent of approval by any other office or employee of the U.S. Government. So my views should not be construed as representing those of the Department of Energy or any other Federal agency.

EIA's latest short term outlook forecast total natural gas consumption average, 71.3 billion cubic feet a day in 2014. That's a slight drop from 2013 as power generators respond to a year over year increase in natural gas prices.

In 2015 forecast natural gas consumption again falls slightly as a decline in residential and commercial use more than offsets increased demand from industry and electricity generation.

On the supply side, EIA forecasts that natural gas marketed production will grow at an average rate of 2 and a half percent in 2014 and more than 1 percent in 2015. Production growth in the Marcellus formation, centered in Pennsylvania, but also evident in West Virginia, is particularly noteworthy. EIA also expects increased drilling activity in the Haynesville in Louisiana and Arkansas and the Barnett in Texas.

The past winter of prolonged widespread and very cold weather which is continuing throughout the Northeast and throughout much of the United States, has led to a record breaking natural gas withdraw season. EIA expects natural gas inventories at the end of this winter will be at the lowest level in 11 years. However, EIA forecasts for production and consumption indicate that operators will make record high storage injections between April and October in order to substantially rebuild inventory levels.

Growing natural gas production in recent years is already having a significant impact on natural gas trade by displacing some pipeline imports from Canada while enabling increased pipeline exports to Mexico. As world scale domestic natural gas liquefaction plants begin to come on stream, EIA expects the United States to become a net exporter of natural gas beginning later this decade.

Turning to longer term projections presented in EIA's Annual Energy Outlook for 2014, natural gas production from shale gas, tight gas and offshore natural gas resources rose steadily increasing 56 percent between 2012 and 2040 when production reaches 37.6 trillion cubic feet in our reference case. The largest contributor, shale gas, will be over 50 percent of total production at that time with tight gas and offshore gas production also increasing. Alaska's natural gas production rises with the opportunity in the middle of the next decade for liquefied natural gas exports to overseas customers.

The complete AEO 2014, the Annual Energy Outlook, which will be released next month, includes cases that examine uncertainties and alternative assumptions that can substantially change this outlook.

For example, projected natural gas production in 2040 is roughly 10 percent above the reference case level in the high oil price scenario and roughly 20 percent above the reference case level in the high oil and gas resource case. Projected prices and export levels also differ considerably across these cases. As producers develop lower grade resources over time EIA sees the spot price at Henry Hub increasing at about 3.7 percent per year in the reference case from a low of $2.75 million, 275 per million BTU to $7 and 65 cents per million BTU in 2040.

Even so, energy intensive industries in the United States benefit from shale gas as both the availability and price of natural gas are attractive compared to the situation in other world regions. Generators using natural gas are also expected to capture a growing share of total U.S. electricity production.

Turning to natural gas trade, pipeline exports of U.S. natural gas to Mexico grow by 6 percent a year in the reference case and are more than 3 times net pipeline imports from Canada by 2040. From 2012 to 2040 U.S. net exports of LNG increase by 3.5 trillion cubic feet with the remaining volumes originating from export terminals located along the Atlantic and Gulf Coasts along with 800 BCF of LNG originating in Alaska.

Future U.S. LNG exports depend on a number of factors that are difficult to anticipate including price convergence in global natural gas markets, competition with oil, the pace of natural gas supply/growth inside and outside the United States. While the AEO 2014 side cases are not yet completed, projected exports by 2040 in our high oil price case are nearly twice as high as the reference case. LNG exports in the high oil and gas resource case which uses a reference case oil price scenario, but is more optimistic about the size of the resource base and technology advances, falls midway between those in the reference and high oil and gas price cases.

Thank you, Chair Landrieu for the opportunity to testify before the committee.

[The prepared statement of Mr. Sieminski follows:]

PREPARED STATEMENT OF ADAM SIEMINSKI, ADMINISTRATOR, ENERGY INFORMATION ADMINISTRATION, DEPARTMENT OF ENERGY

Chair Landrieu, Ranking Member Murkowski, and Members of the Committee, I appreciate the opportunity to appear before you today at this hearing on the topic of Importing Energy, Exporting Jobs, Can it be Reversed?

The Energy Information Administration (EIA) is the statistical and analytical agency within the U.S. Department of Energy. EIA collects, analyzes, and disseminates independent and impartial energy information to promote sound policymaking, efficient markets, and public understanding regarding energy and its interaction with the economy and the environment. EIA is the nation's premier source of energy information and, by law, its data, analyses, and forecasts are independent of approval by any other officer or employee of the United States Government. The views expressed herein should therefore not be construed as representing those of the Department of Energy or any other federal agency.

As requested, my testimony focuses on natural gas. It draws on EIA's data covering production, stocks, demand, imports, exports, and prices; on our forecast of trends over the next one to two years that is updated each month in the Short-term Energy Outlook (STEO). It also draws on long-term projections through 2040 that are updated each year in our Annual Energy Outlook (AEO), including a variety of alternative cases to reflect the effect of key uncertainties on energy market outcomes.

6

Short Term: U.S. Natural Gas Production, Use and Trade

This winter of prolonged, widespread frigid weather throughout much of the United States led to a record-breaking natural gas withdrawal season, bringing inventories of natural gas to an 11-year low at the end of the current winter. EIA's weekly natural gas storage report issued on March 20 shows that stocks as of March 14 were 953 Billion cubic feet (Bcf). However, EIA forecasts for production and consumption indicate that operators will make record-high storage injections between April and October in order to substantially rebuild inventory levels. The demand response to higher natural gas prices should be particularly apparent in the electric power sector, where decisions made by operators regarding which power plants to run during shoulder demand periods are quite sensitive to relative fuel prices.

EIA expects total natural gas consumption will average 71.3 Bcf per day (Bcf/d) in 2014, a drop of 0.1 Bcf/d from 2013. The projected year-over-year increases in natural gas prices contribute to declines in natural gas used for electric power generation from 24.9 Bcf/d in 2012 to 22.3 Bcf/d in 2013 and 22.0 Bcf/d in 2014. In 2015, total natural gas consumption falls by 0.3 Bcf/d as a decline in residential and commercial consumption more than offsets consumption growth in the industrial and electric power sectors. EIA expects natural gas consumption in the power sector to increase to 22.6 Bcf/d in 2015 with the retirement of some coal plants.

Total marketed production averaged 70.2 billion cubic feet per day in 2013. The latest STEO forecasts natural gas marketed production to grow at an average rate of 2.5 percent in 2014 and 1.1 percent in 2015. U.S. natural gas production has increased significantly since 2005 mainly because of growth in production of shale gas resources. The recent rapid natural gas production growth in the Marcellus formation, centered in Pennsylvania, but also evident in West Virginia, is particularly noteworthy. Supply growth in the Northeast is causing natural gas forward prices in that region to fall even with or below Henry Hub prices outside of peak-demand winter months. Consequently, some drilling activity may again shift towards Gulf Coast plays such as the Haynesville in Louisiana and the Barnett in Texas, where prices are closer to the Henry Hub spot prices.

Turning to natural gas trade, growing domestic production over the past several years has displaced some pipeline imports from Canada, while exports to Mexico have increased. EIA expects these trends will continue through 2015. EIA projects net natural gas imports of 3.6 Bcf/d in 2014 and 2.6 Bcf/d in 2015, which would be the lowest level since 1987. The latest AEO, which is discussed below, projects the United States will be a net exporter of natural gas beginning later in this decade.

The Long Term Outlook for U.S. Natural Gas

EIA released the Reference case projections for the Annual Energy Outlook 20014 (AEO2014) in December. The Reference case is intended to represent an energy future through 2040 based on given market, technological, and demographic trends; current laws and regulations; and consumer behavior. EIA recognizes that projections of energy markets are highly uncertain and subject to geopolitical disruptions, technological breakthroughs, economic fluctuations, and other unforeseeable events. In addition, long-term trends in technology development, demographics, economic growth, and energy resources may evolve along a different path than represented in the Reference case projections. The complete AEO2014, which will be released next month, includes a number of alternative cases that examine uncertainties and alternative assumptions regarding resources, technology advances, and world energy prices that can significantly affect projections for natural gas production, use, and trade.

In the AEO2014 Reference case, natural gas production grows steadily, with a 56 percent increase between 2012 and 2040, when production reaches 37.6 trillion cubic feet (Tcf). Shale gas production is the largest contributor, growing by more than 10 Tcf, from 9.7 Tcf in 2012 to 19.8 Tcf in 2040. The shale gas share of total U.S. natural gas production increases to over 50 percent. Tight gas production and offshore gas production both increase significantly, but their share of total production remains relatively constant. Alaska's natural gas production also increases during the projection period, driven by the opportunity for Alaska liquefied natural gas (LNG) exports to overseas customers, which is projected to be economic in the middle of the next decade.

One key uncertainty that influences projected U.S. natural gas production is the level of oil prices, relative to natural gas prices, which significantly affects projected use of natural gas in the transportation sector and projected foreign demand for U.S. natural gas exports. A second key uncertainty influencing projected domestic natural gas production relates to the abundance of tight oil and shale gas resources and the pace of technology advances that influence both drilling costs and the recovery factor. The impact of alternative assumptions in these two areas will be explored

7

in AEO2014 side cases that address high and low oil price scenarios and more optimistic and pessimistic assumptions regarding the resource base and the pace of technology advances. The impacts of revised assumptions and scenarios can be substantial. For example, projected natural gas production in 2040 is roughly 4 Tcf above the Reference case level in the High Oil Price scenario, and roughly 8 Tcf above the Reference case level in the High Oil and Gas Resource case. Projected prices and export levels also differ considerably across these cases.

Average annual U.S. natural gas prices have remained relatively low over the past several years as a result of the availability of abundant domestic resources and the application of improved production technologies. Growth in demand for natural gas, largely from the electric power and industrial sectors (including oil refineries), and for LNG exports, supports higher prices, particularly toward the end of the present decade. To meet that rising demand, producers move into basins where the recovery of natural gas is more difficult and expensive, which leads to an increase in Henry Hub spot prices of 3.7 percent per year in the Reference case, from $2.75 per million Btu (MMbtu) in 2012 to $7.65 per MMbtu (2012 dollars) in 2040.

Energy intensive Industries benefit from shale gas

Availability of natural gas and hydrocarbon gas liquids (HGL) from wet gas production at prices that are attractive relative to those in other regions supports the growth of energy intensive industries that rely on those as both a fuel and as a feedstock in the United States.

Overall, industrial shipments grow at a 3.0 percent annual rate over the first 10 years of the AEO2014 Reference case projection and then slow to 1.6 percent annual growth from 2025 through 2040. Bulk chemicals and metals-based durables account for much of the increased growth in industrial shipments in AEO2014. Industrial shipments of bulk chemicals, which benefit from an increased supply of natural gas liquids, grow by 3.4 percent per year from 2012 to 2025 in AEO2014. The higher level of industrial shipments leads to more natural gas consumption in the U.S. industrial sector, increasing from 8.7 quadrillion British thermal units (Btu) in 2012 to 10.6 quadrillion Btu in 2025 in AEO2014, compared to 9.8 quadrillion Btu in 2025 in AEO2013. Natural gas use in manufacturing, the single largest component of overall industrial gas use, rises rapidly over the next decade. Projected prices for natural gas also make it a very attractive fuel for new generating capacity. In 2040, natural gas accounts for 35 percent of total electricity generation, while coal accounts for 32 percent.

Growth in Transportation Demand and Exports

Some of the largest changes in consumption are seen for natural gas consumed in transportation and exported as LNG, since the profitability of natural gas as transportation fuel or as LNG for export depends primarily on the price differential between crude oil and natural gas. Although transportation use currently accounts for only a small portion of total U.S. natural gas consumption, the percentage growth in natural gas demand by heavy-duty vehicles, ships, and trains is significant. Consumption in the transportation sector, excluding natural gas use at compressor stations, grows from about 40 billion cubic feet in 2012 to 850 billion cubic feet in 2040.

U.S. exports of natural gas also increase in the AEO2014 Reference case. Pipeline exports of U.S. natural gas to Mexico grow by 6 percent per year, from 0.6 Tcf in 2012 to 3.1 Tcf in 2040. Over the same period, as more U.S. demand is met by domestic production, net pipeline imports from Canada fall to less than 1 Tcf. From 2012 to 2040, U.S. net exports of LNG increase by 3.5 Tcf, including 800 Bcf of LNG originating in Alaska, with the remaining volumes originating from export terminals located along the Atlantic and Gulf coasts. In general, future U.S. LNG exports depend on a number of factors that are difficult to anticipate, including the speed and extent of price convergence in global natural gas markets, the extent to which natural gas competes with oil in U.S. and international gas markets, and the pace of natural gas supply growth outside the United States.

Projected U.S. natural gas exports are sensitive to the abundance of tight oil and shale gas resources, the pace of technology advances that influences drilling costs, the recovery factor, and evolution of global oil prices. While the AEO2014 side cases are not yet completed, projected LNG exports by 2040 in the High Oil Price case are nearly twice as high as in the Reference case. Projected LNG exports in the High Oil and Gas Resource case, which uses the Reference case oil price scenario but is more optimistic about the size of the resource base and technology advance, fall midway between those in the Reference and High Oil Price cases.

Thank you for the opportunity to testify before the Committee.

The CHAIR. Thank you very much.

Please proceed.

STATEMENT OF W. DAVID MONTGOMERY, PH.D., NERA, ECONOMIC CONSULTING

Mr. MONTGOMERY. Thank you, Madame Chair. I thought you were going to ask questions of Mr. Sieminski.

The CHAIR. No, no. We do the whole panel. Then we'll have questions.

Mr. MONTGOMERY. Thank you.

Madame Chair and members of the committee, I'm also honored by your invitation to testify today in this distinguished company. It was my privilege to lead the study of the macro economic impacts of U.S. LNG exports that my company, National Economic Research Associates, did for the Department of Energy and of our recent update to that study. I've provided a copy of the updated report along with my testimony. I'd like to request that that be entered into the record.

The CHAIR. Without objection.

Mr. MONTGOMERY. Thank you.

My testimony and these reports represent my own opinions and conclusions and do not necessarily represent the opinions of any other consultant at NERA or its clients and in particular, I do not speak for Cheniere Energy which funded the update or for NERA, but only for myself. We tried to address some issues that have been raised about our earlier study for DOE in this update.

Two, in particular, one that using 2011 data made our study too out of date, well we updated it to the Energy Information Administration's most recent full set of long term forecasts. We used the 2013 outlook because, as Mr. Sieminski just said, they have not yet published the side cases that were critical for our analysis of the scenarios. We agree with Mr. Sieminski that we have to look at scenarios because it is very difficult to predict exactly what the level of exports will be.

Then to deal with concerns that DOE does not have access to a full analysis of the cumulative impacts of exports we examined levels of exports all the way up to what they could be if the Department of Energy put no restrictions on exports. We again found that LNG exports provide net economic benefits in all the scenarios we examined, the greater the exports, the greater the benefits. Put another way, there's no sweet spot that would justify limiting LNG exports below market determined levels on the basis of their net economic benefits.

Another point that's been raised frequently is about the notion that somehow if we export natural gas it won't be available for manufacturing in the U.S. That's simply a false dichotomy. We looked at it very closely.

You're absolutely right, Madame Chair, the U.S. chemicals industry was very threatened in 2005. But at this point it has moved to being tied for the world's lowest cost producer of chemicals with a very large advantage over any of its rivals that import natural gas which will not be taken away to any noticeable extent by the effect of LNG exports. It's simply a false dichotomy.

There is ample gas for both. We find that in fact in our scenarios the increased demand for exports is almost all satisfied by increased production. None of it, almost none of it is taken away from any domestic uses because of higher prices.

I'd like to cover 2 other topics.

One, just extending the economic analysis to talk about jobs. There are 2 things about LNG exports that I am convinced are true no matter what level of exports we look at.

First is that LNG export facilities in shale gas production require workers. They're going to be drawn from all over the economy. Since the facilities have to be built before the gas can be loaded the investment in employment associated with that investment is going to be coming up front.

We calculated, this is on page 8 of my testimony, and I believe the committee may have a handout. We calculated the annual employment, just direct jobs, building liquefaction facilities. Those jobs could hit a peak between 2,000 and 30,000 jobs onsite building liquefaction facilities between now and 2018. Of course the faster we export gas, the more jobs there will be. The faster we get going on exporting gas, building the facilities, the more jobs there will be.

I mentioned the year 2018 because I think it's really important. The Congressional Budget Office, where I used to be an Assistant Director, does economic forecasts for the budget. It always assumes that the economy will be back at full employment after we come out of the current cycle simply because we can't do any better than that at forecasting what will happen. It has been the long term secular trend in the economy.

So what's really important about employment is the period between now and when we reach full employment which CBO now projects for 2018. So these jobs are actually coming exactly when they're needed, which is during a period when we are still looking at unemployed workers, who can be brought back into the labor force. We project that somewhere between 2,000 and 45,000 unemployed would be put back to work between now and 2018 by the construction of these, by basically, the entire enterprise of gearing up for LNG exports.

The final point I would like to make is about Russia which we all are, really, the focus of this hearing.

I've looked at our new study and asked myself what is it that is effective and sufficiently attractive on its own merits that would be a credible promise of punishment for Russian aggression?

I believe that that is LNG exports. If you look quickly at another handout that I believe you have or on page 13 of my testimony. We've taken a look at what would happen to Russia's revenues if 2 things happened.

One of them is we've removed, you know, a policy, you know, however it is actually phrased in law, that committed the U.S. not to put a cap on LNG exports combined with putting serious effort into being sure that we do not cutoff the shale gas revolution through ham handed regulation or giving in to, you know, groundless fears and encourage production. Those 2 things together are needed.

But with that we could see Russia's exports dropping by up to 5 trillion cubic feet per year in 2038 due to this competition from the U.S. That's what would happen if Russia does not meet the prices that the U.S and other competitive producers. We would take away a huge amount of their market.

If they do meet the competition they're going to have to sell at lower prices. What that adds up to me in this chart is somewhere between a 40 percent and a 60 percent loss in export revenues from natural gas for Russia through this policy of the U.S. entering the LNG market aggressively. I think that's a punishment that would mean something.

Thank you.

[The prepared statement of Mr. Montgomery follows:]

PREPARED STATEMENT OF W. DAVID MONTGOMERY, PH.D., NERA ECONOMIC CONSULTING

Chairman Landrieu, Ranking Member Murkowski and Members of the Committee:

Introduction

I am honored by your invitation to testify on this very important topic. I am an economist and Senior Vice President at NERA Economic Consulting. I had the privilege of leading the study of the "Macroeconomic Impacts of U.S. LNG Exports" that was issued by the Department of Energy (DOE) in December 2012 and of the update to that study, "Updated Macroeconomic Impacts of LNG Exports from the United States," that my colleagues and I have just completed. I have provided a copy of this report along with my testimony and I request that it be entered into the record. I would like to thank Cheniere Energy, Inc. for their sponsorship of this update, and in particular to thank them for giving us the same freedom to conduct an objective and independent study that the U.S. Department of Energy gave us.

Statements in this testimony represent my own opinions and conclusions and do not necessarily represent opinions of any other consultant at NERA or any of its clients. I do not speak for Cheniere Energy, Inc. or NERA, in particular, but only for myself.

Findings of the NERA 2014 Study

We based our updated analysis on the Energy Information Agency's (EIA) 2013 Annual Energy Outlook (AEO 2013), in order to address claims that our original study was out of date. Compared to our 2012 report, natural gas prices are lower, LNG exports are larger, and economic benefits are greater. We again find that LNG exports provide net economic benefits in all scenarios, and the less regulators restrict U.S. exports, the greater the benefits from natural gas production.

We used AEO 2013 in this update because the preliminary release of AEO 2014 did not contain the side cases exploring high and low oil and gas resources that were needed to recapitulate the scenarios of our 2012 study. I do not expect our findings to change when we incorporate AEO 2014 scenarios because when we jumped forward two years from AEO 2011 to AEO 2013 everything became more favorable to LNG exports: lower U.S. natural gas prices, higher LNG exports and greater economic benefits in every case.

In order to address concerns about the "cumulative" impact of LNG exports above levels that DOE asked us to study, our update considers additional scenarios in which we assume no constraints on LNG exports and let the market determine their level. These scenarios of LNG exports unconstrained by government policy provided the largest net benefits.

Another goal that we had in this update was to dispel some myths that are still being retold about natural gas exports, and I will turn to them now:

LNG exports will not cause runaway increases in natural gas prices.—Both LNG export volumes and price impacts will be limited by the market, by rival exporters ready to undercut high prices, and by price-sensitive buyers. Only if natural gas prices fall and remain below today's levels will there be high levels of exports. If regulatory ham-handedness chokes off the shale revolution, not even the currently authorized LNG export projects will be running. The U.S. would not find buyers at high prices for large volumes of LNG exports, even with extraordinary global demand and supply shocks. There are too many other sellers that can beat high U.S. prices.

Exhibit 1* shows the impact of LNG exports on U.S. natural gas prices with EIA Reference Case supply assumptions and a global demand shock[1] for unconstrained exports. The historical variation in prices around their mean from 2000 to 2013 is superimposed on projected natural gas prices and their mean from 2025 to 2038. We can see that the difference of less than $1 is dwarfed by historical variations.

Exhibit 1—Price Impacts of LNG Exports Are Dwarfed by Historical Variation

Exhibit 2 shows the maximum increase in natural gas prices that we find across all scenarios to be about $1 per Mcf. In contrast, the difference in natural gas prices between EIA's High Oil and Gas Resource (HOGR) case and its Low Oil and Gas Resource (LOGR) case is over $3.50. We find that natural gas prices as high as in the LOGR case would choke off LNG exports at levels less than what DOE has already authorized.

Exhibit 2—Price Impacts of LNG Exports, Limited Shale Development, and Winter Weather

Price spikes will not become more damaging.—Returning to our own analysis, short term natural gas price spikes, as we observed last winter, have been a frequent occurrence in natural gas markets even with zero LNG exports. They are caused by unexpected weather events and problems in the pipeline system, and have always been temporary. Referring again to Exhibit 1, Henry Hub prices that rose to almost $8.00/Mcf last winter are already down to $4.50. There has always been a solution for price spikes: which is increased storage and overbuilding of the pipeline system. But neither natural gas suppliers nor their customers have found the permanent cost of this extra security worth the temporary cost of price spikes.

LNG exports actually provide a deliverability cushion for domestic consumers. Our analysis shows that when U.S. wellhead prices become as high as they were last winter, they would likely choke off LNG exports and free up that gas for domestic use. The additional natural gas deliverability built up to serve LNG exports would then become available to surge deliveries for domestic needs. Thus LNG exports provide a built in buffer of supply like a Strategic Petroleum Reserve.

Limiting LNG exports would take away this deliverability cushion, and the disastrous consequences of past governmental attempts to allocate supplies and control prices during price spikes should be a warning against trying again. Natural gas prices were regulated through the 1970s, and the consequence was an allocation system that cut off major users—mostly industrial customers—when shortages appeared. Decisions by government regulators and politicians about who should be awarded the benefits of price-controlled gas just made things worse for everyone. There have been no such curtailments since we created an open market for natural gas in the U.S.

Natural gas will not be taken away from U.S. manufacturing or residential consumers to supply LNG exports.—LNG exports occur precisely because there is enough natural gas to satisfy needs inside and outside the U.S. We consistently find that most of the demand for increased natural gas exports is satisfied by new production, and that demand reduction is largely confined to the electric power sector (Exhibit 3).

In the electric power sector, an increased price of natural gas as a fuel for generation would lead to a small reduction in demand, but for the most part natural gas is displaced by additional generation from nuclear, renewables, and (depending on forthcoming EPA rules) possibly coal.

Exhibit 3—Where Do Exports Come From?

The competitive advantage of U.S. manufacturing will not be taken away, at least not by LNG exports.—Right now U.S. chemical producers enjoy about a 4 to 1 cost advantage over their rivals in Europe and Asia. Exhibit 4 from the American Chemical Council shows how the competitive position of this sector has become fundamentally invulnerable to effects of LNG exports. For ethylene, an important bulk chemical and indicator of competitiveness used by the American Chemical Council, costs in the U.S. are about 20 cents per pound and in China and Europe over 80 cents per pound. The maximum impact that LNG exports could have on U.S. natural gas prices would raise costs in the U.S. by about 5 cents per pound—still leaving a 55 cent per pound cost advantage.

Exhibit 4—Competitive Position of U.S. Chemical Industry

For ethylene producers, the picture is even rosier because their primary feedstock, ethane, is a natural gas liquid that is produced in large quantities along with tight

---

*All Exhibits have been retained in committee files.
[1] The demand shock assumes greater international demand for natural gas than assumed in the 2013 International Energy Outlook.

gas. Ethane is so "hot" that the amount that can be mixed into natural gas in pipelines is limited, so that a glut of ethane has developed over the past two years and lowered the price of ethane relative to natural gas. And, the more LNG we export, the greater the glut of ethane will be and the greater the advantage to chemical producers.

All U.S. manufacturing continues to enjoy a cushion of low natural gas costs no matter how high LNG exports go. Any importer of natural gas from the U.S. will be paying a landed price more than twice the price that U.S. manufacturers pay—because the cost of transporting gas to Europe or Asia is about equal to the price of gas in the U.S. Adding the two together means that rivals importing gas from the U.S. will be paying double the U.S. price. As a result, we find across all sectors and in all scenarios that LNG exports alter the rate of growth in U.S. manufacturing by no more than a few hundredths of a percentage point.

And at that, natural gas will be a bargain to the countries that import from the U.S. LNG imports in Asia and pipeline imports into Europe from Russia are now for the most part indexed to oil prices. That makes the current price of natural gas 3 to 4 times higher in those countries than in the U.S. That is what makes the prospect of LNG exports so attractive to both buyers and sellers, and why LNG exports from the U.S. are such a threat to Russia.

LNG exports will not cost U.S. jobs.—Just the construction of liquefaction capacity sufficient to support the LNG exports projected in our study would create a peak of 2000 to 40,000 onsite jobs, largely in the Gulf Coast region and in the critical years between now and 2018 (Exhibit 5). That year is important, because it is the year when CBO forecasts that the U.S. will return to a normal state of full employment. The investment in LNG export facilities and in additional natural gas exploration and production for export would take from 3,000 to 45,000 workers off the unemployment rolls during the next four years of continued softness in the labor market, and hasten the return to full employment by as much as two months. The faster projects are authorized and the sooner they begin construction, the greater the impact on unemployment will be.

Exhibit 5—Eployment Impacts

Benefits of LNG exports will be distributed broadly.—Employment, labor income and investment income will continue to grow no matter what level of LNG exports the market demands from the U.S. In the scenario with the highest level of LNG exports across all those we examined, GDP in 2038 will increase by about $25 billion compared to the no export case. In terms of the components of GDP, government revenues will increase by over $10 billion, investment income by about $15 billion, and resource income by about $10 billion, and labor income will be about $15 billion less, all compared to the no export case.

Exhibit 6—LNG Exports Lead to Higher GDP

There is no point in turning these findings into class warfare. A considerably larger share of royalty income could accrue to the Federal government if more Federal lands opened up for oil and gas exploration and production, and that would in turn likely reduce resource income to private landowners. The increase in investment income more than offsets a decline in wage income, and that increase plus a share of resource income will accrue to all Americans who invest and who hold their 401k plans in a reasonably diversified portfolio of stocks.

There is no "sweet spot" lower than the market-determined level of exports—Finally, we found no sweet spot that would justify government interference with U.S. obligations under the WTO to allow free trade in commodities like natural gas. In every scenario we investigated, higher levels of LNG exports led to larger economic benefits to the U.S. (See Exhibit 7).

Exhibit 7—When the Market Decides, the More We Export, the More We Benefit

We examined a range of LNG exports in our study, including market-determined levels of exports that could be expected if DOE automatically approved all applications. Even in cases where worldwide supply and demand shocks were combined with optimistic assumptions about U.S. natural gas resources to lead to LNG exports approaching one-half of total domestic supply, the U.S. gained larger benefits by allowing unlimited LNG exports than it would have achieved in those cases with restricted exports

Strategic Energy Policy

Now let me turn to the subject of this hearing. LNG exports from the U.S. could reduce Russia's stranglehold on energy supplies to Europe. Immediate announcement of a policy of allowing unlimited LNG exports would signal potential competition that Russia would have to meet by offering lower natural gas prices as it renegotiates its supply contracts with Europe. The power of this signal will depend on whether it is accompanied by effective action to accelerate the shale gas revolution by avoiding or removing unreasonable regulations, costs, and constraints on natural gas exploration and production.

In order to estimate the potential demand for U.S. LNG exports and the prices at which LNG exports could be sold, we analyzed supply and demand for natural gas around the world. Russia supplies about 25 percent of the natural gas consumed in Europe and Russian exports are projected by EIA to increase by 33 Bcfd from current levels by 2040, making Russia the largest potential rival to the U.S. in global LNG supply. Much of this gas is now supplied by Russia under long term contracts that link natural gas prices to oil prices. As these contracts come up for renewal or renegotiation, Russia's power to extract high prices will depend greatly on the competition expected to appear in the market during that contract term.

Monopolists can be restrained as effectively by potential competition as by actual production by their rivals. Eliminating any possibility of a cap on U.S. exports is necessary to create effective potential competition. The existence of a major competitor with the capacity and willingness to sell large quantities of natural gas will discipline Russia's pricing even if actual LNG exports are low. To provide such competition, it must be possible to move additional LNG exports into the market on a large enough scale to punish any Russian effort to raise prices above competitive levels with a substantial loss of market share.

Our results show that if U.S. policies encourage growth in natural gas production and remove all limits on exports, Russia would face the choice of ceding a large share of its market to the U.S. and other rivals or lowering its prices to levels determined by gas-on-gas competition. Even if it takes 5 to 10 years for U.S. LNG exports to equal a large share of Russian natural gas exports, the effect of a clear policy to encourage domestic oil and gas production and remove obstacles to LNG exports would have an immediate effect on the pricing of natural gas and Russia's revenues.

To be specific, I would like to refer to Exhibit 8. The shows the range of impacts that a policy of unlimited U.S. LNG exports could have on Russia's natural gas export revenues if shale gas resources and regulatory policy toward drilling lead to levels of production approximating the most recent EIA High Oil and Gas Resource case. Since U.S. LNG exports will affect Russian pipeline as well as LNG exports, these estimates of Russia's revenues include both pipeline and waterborne shipments. The U.S. need not be competing directly with Russia for U.S. exports to have the effect of reducing Russia's exports and revenues. Even if U.S. exports move to Asia, they would divert LNG to Europe and thus take away Russia's sales and revenues.

Exhibit 8—Effective U.S. Competition Would Force Russia to Cut Prices or Lose Sales

Thus, we estimate that in the next 5 years, U.S. competition could drive Russia's revenues from natural gas exports down by as much as 30 percent, and in the longer term could cut those revenues by as much as 60 percent. Since energy exports are the mainstay of the still inefficient and lagging Russian economy, this is a penalty with teeth. LNG exports will not alone be sufficient to discipline Russian aggression, but it is a step in the right direction.

A likely consequence of high levels of U.S. LNG exports based on Henry Hub prices lower than today is that they could break the system of oil-linked pricing by which Russia has enriched itself at Europe's expense. This outbreak of gas-on-gas competition is a major part of the erosion of Russia's export revenues found in our results, and it would limit Russia's energy and economic power.

Gas-on-gas competition will also benefit U.S. consumers by lowering costs of manufacturing in countries that import natural gas, and thereby lowering the cost of consumer goods imported from those regions. This reduction in costs of our trade partners can only benefit the U.S. consumer, but it may be opposed by some manufacturing interests. The outbreak of gas-on-gas competition may erode further the profits of U.S. chemical producers that I discussed earlier, by bringing their rivals' costs for feedstocks down closer to U.S. levels. The competitive advantage of the U.S. will not disappear because the U.S. as an exporter will have natural gas prices half those that importers must pay to obtain LNG plus shipping. But the profits of some of those U.S. chemical producers could be eroded, by the same events that provide U.S. consumers with the benefit of lower prices of many other imported goods and the world with a meaningful counter to Russian aggression.

Since oil, natural gas, and coal markets in Europe are linked, exports of any of the three energy forms could contribute to weakening Russia's power over Europe and eroding its export revenues. By increasing coal exports to Europe, the U.S. would likely displace natural gas used for power generation in Europe and thereby allow either more rapid refilling of European storage or directly cut back needs for

Russian natural gas. Crude oil exports might not directly compete with Russian supplies to Europe, but to the extent that crude oil exports make greater U.S. production possible they would shift the global supply-demand balance toward excess supply and put downward pressure globally on oil prices. This would then reduce Russia's oil export revenues. The combined loss of oil and natural gas export revenue would further weaken the Russian economy and its ability to finance military expansion, and uneconomic withholding of energy supplies to blackmail its neighbors. Much as the efforts of the Soviet Union to match U.S. military strength in the 1980s broke its centrally planned economy and led to the downfall of communism, U.S. energy strength fostered by a strategic commitment to production and exports could ultimately break Russia's energy dominance and restrain its revanchist ambitions.

Like the victory over Communism, these changes will take years. The FERC process for approving export terminals will remain, and market conditions and financing will stretch out construction. The fears promoted by some that the entire 8 Bcf/day of capacity approved by DOE to date to non-FTA countries will appear overnight and suddenly drain the U.S. of natural gas are entirely unfounded. There will be an immediate effect on Russia's ability to hold up European customers for oil linked prices in long term contracts, because of the potential competition of U.S. exporters and the expectation that U.S. entry into the global market could wreck the oil-based pricing system. It is also true that Russia's exports to Europe will not be replaced overnight, but countering the Russian Anschluss is not the only reason for removing limits on LNG exports.

However rapidly LNG exports actually grow over the next few years, a strategy of maximizing U.S. oil and natural gas production by removing unreasonable constraints and obstacles and of pre-authorizing exports without any quantitative cap will have a long run effect of weakening the Russian economy. The Cold War lasted for 50 years before the economic superiority of the Free World defeated Communism, and a long view is necessary to resist what appears to be resurgent Russian nationalism and territorial expansion. Fortunately, that long strategic view is in this case in line with U.S. immediate economic interests, which are served best by removing limits on LNG exports.

The CHAIR. Thank you, Doctor.

Mr. Goldwyn.

Then I'm going to come back to the Minister at the end and let this group go first. Thank you.

Mr. Goldwyn.

STATEMENT OF DAVID L. GOLDWYN, NONRESIDENT SENIOR FELLOW, BROOKINGS INSTITUTION, AND PRESIDENT, GOLDWYN GLOBAL STRATEGIES, LLC

Mr. GOLDWYN. Great. Thank you, madame chair and ranking member and members of the committee for this opportunity to be here today and with my distinguished panelists. I also speak on my own behalf and not for Brookings.

The dramatic growth in natural gas reserves and production in the United States over the last 5 years has resulted in economic growth, relative reductions in greenhouse gas emissions and greater energy security. Every credible estimate of our future energy supply suggests we will have exportable surpluses of natural gas for decades to come. This bounty could enhance our national power by positioning our Nation as a reliable supplier of natural gas to regions of the world that suffer from intimidation from their suppliers or simply the economy crushing burden of oil linked prices.

The question before us is not whether we have this geopolitical potential, but whether we will realize it in time to help our friends and allies.

Countries enhance their national power when they act as reliable suppliers of strategic commodities to the global market. This power can be wielded for good to stabilize markets and create competitive prices. But it can also be wielded for ill as we have seen with Russia using its market power to intimidate its neighbors.

The U.S. can be a strategic supplier to the global gas market.

While our government doesn't dictate where that supply will go it does control how fast we will connect to the global market. The Natural Gas Act has inadvertently put our friends and allies, those who don't have free trade agreements with us, at the back of the line. In addition the process and the tempo for reviewing these exports to LNG counties that we don't have free trade agreements with is potentially out of sync with commercial realities.

The crisis in Ukraine should cause us to think anew on this process. See if we can leverage our natural gas bounty to help our allies by accelerating the consideration of export applications so they can plan for the day when they can reduce their reliance on Russian gas or on the oil linked prices that are crippling their economies. In addition we should begin now to compete actively with Russia for Asia's markets before we see that region as well to dependence on Russian supply.

While the benefits of U.S. LNG exports would be global, my remarks will focus on Europe because of the crisis in Ukraine. Also—they also reflect an article that I published for Brookings which I'd also like to enter into the record.

Russia's annexation of Crimea illustrates both the challenge and opportunity that we face. The challenge is grave. This Russian challenge will be with us as long as President Putin remains in power. His unabashed desire to recover territories that became independent after the fall of the Soviet Union is a threat to European security and to American leadership.

The President has responded, I think, with savvy and with skill by targeting the kleptocratic inner circle that tries to use Russia's private, well, public resources for private gain.

But Russia's neighbors, especially the Nations of Central and Eastern Europe remain dependent on Russian gas and Russian oil linked supplies. Now to address its energy insecurity Europe has to do a lot on its own.

It needs to make strides toward further integrating its gas markets so it can move from point to point.

It needs to promote internal market reform in member countries so someone would want to invest there.

It needs to develop further infrastructure to support alternative gas supply, interconnections among member countries and indigenous gas development.

The U.S. will also need to recommit to our Caspian policy to ensure that the southern corridor is completed and that Azerbaijan and Kazakhstan maintain their autonomy and sustain their roles as suppliers of oil and gas to Europe. We can make further integration of Europe's gas markets a key tenant of our engagement as well. But a clear signal from the U.S. that LNG exports will be available to European allies for future purchase would put immediate pressure on Russia's market share and would also help accelerate investment in and construction of gas transportation infrastructure in Europe.

Their LNG import project is tabled in Lithuania, Ukraine, Poland, Croatia and Estonia. There are interconnections planned to move gas to Poland, Latvia and Finland.

While it's no panacea and I don't profess that it is, removing the uncertainty as to whether and when U.S. LNG export projects that contract with European empires can get that approval will accelerate both the financing of U.S. LNG export projects and European import projects. Those who dismiss the utility of accelerating these approvals underestimate the impact it can have on eroding Russia's market power now. We signal the availability of Henry Hub LNG pricing it impacts price formation for the future and erodes the price Russia can get for its gas in Europe and Asia. Reducing Russia's market share in Europe makes its companies less attractive and investment in its upstream less valuable.

Witness the fall in the prices of Novatek just after we announced sanctions. Markets react today to news in the future.

Finally, allowing European LNG projects to access Henry Hub pricing makes those projects more financeable. It may be true that Asian buyers rather than European buyers buy U.S. LNG. But from a geopolitical perspective it doesn't make a difference. Eroding Russia's Asian market share and pricing power also hurts their cash-flow. The more U.S. Henry Hub priced gas hits the market, the greater the bargaining power of European buyers.

So, as I said at the outset, these are serious times that call for serious solutions. Having a refreshed European energy security policy and accelerated U.S. LNG exports are part of that tool box. They may be long term measures, but they're serious measures. The time to get started is now.

[The prepared statement of Mr. Goldwyn follows:]

STATEMENT OF DAVID L. GOLDWYN, NONRESIDENT SENIOR FELLOW, BROOKINGS INSTITUTION, AND PRESIDENT, GOLDWYN GLOBAL STRATEGIES, LLC

THE ROLE OF NATURAL GAS EXPORTS IN U.S. FOREIGN POLICY

Madam Chairwoman and Members of the Committee, it is an honor to speak with you today about the geopolitical benefits of America's natural gas bounty. The dramatic growth in natural gas reserves and production in the United States over the past five years has resulted in economic growth, relative reductions in greenhouse gas emissions, and greater energy security. Every credible estimate of our energy future suggests we will have substantial exportable surpluses of natural gas for decades to come. This bounty could enhance our national power by positioning our nation as a reliable supplier of natural gas to regions of the world that suffer from intimidation from their suppliers or simply the economy crushing burden of oil linked prices. The question before us is not whether we have this geopolitical potential, but whether we will realize it in time to help our friends and allies.

Several reports and studies have established a consensus that the benefits of liquefied natural gas (LNG) exports from the U.S. significantly outweigh the costs. As the co-chair of the Brookings Institution Natural Gas Task Force, we explored many of the issues surrounding LNG exports. Following the completion of the Task Force sessions, my colleagues at Brookings published a well-received report that found that price impacts of LNG exports would be minimal, and that the effects of LNG export on the U.S. gross domestic product and trade balance would be positive[1] The macroeconomic LNG study commissioned by the Department of Energy, prepared by

---

[1] Charles Ebinger, Kevin Massy, and Govinda Avasarala, "Liquid Markets: Assessing the Case for U.S. Exports of Liquefied Natural Gas," Brookings Institution, May 2012, p. xiii. (Ebinger, 2012)

NERA Economic Consulting,[2] found that there would be net economic benefits to the U.S. at all levels of exports modeled. Just last month, NERA released an update to that study which added several new scenarios,[3] once again finding that "LNG exports provide net economic benefits in all the scenarios investigated, and the greater the level of exports, the greater the benefits."[4]

I am here today to speak about the foreign policy benefits that LNG exports can provide. Countries enhance their national power when they act as reliable suppliers of strategic commodities to the global market. This power can be wielded for good, to stabilize markets and create competitive prices. It can also be used for ill, as we have seen with Russia, using its market power to intimidate its neighbors. The U.S. can be a strategic supplier to the global gas market. While our government does not dictate where that supply will go, it does control how fast we will connect to the global market. The Natural Gas Act has inadvertently put the friends and allies who need us most at the back of the line. The process for reviewing exports of LNG to countries we do not have free trade agreements with has proven to be cumbersome, and potentially out of sync with commercial realities.

The crisis in Ukraine should cause us to think anew on this process and see if we can leverage our natural gas bounty to help our allies by accelerating the consideration of export applications so that they can plan for the day when they can reduce their reliance on Russian gas or on the oil-linked prices that are crippling their economies. In addition, we should begin now to compete actively with Russia for Asia's markets before we cede that region as well to dependence on Russian supply.

While the benefits of U.S. LNG exports would be global, my remarks will focus on the impact to Europe in light of the current crisis in Ukraine. I will briefly address the implications for Asia towards the end of my testimony. My remarks today reflect an article that I published just last week at the Brookings Institution,[5] which I will also submit for the record.

If the U.S. were to accelerate the consideration of exports to non-FTA countries, by allowing projects that have received environmental clearance to receive expedited consideration,[6] or by agreeing to consider all projects with environmental clearance from the Federal Energy Regulatory Commission (FERC) within 90 days of receiving that clearance,[7] or more broadly by deeming exports of LNG to all countries to be in the national interest,[8] the energy security of import dependent countries like Japan and the nations of Central and Eastern Europe would be improved. Expectations of future supply drive energy prices and impact infrastructure investment decisions made today. While no panacea, U.S. LNG exports would have a significant impact on global markets for natural gas and the energy security of some of our closest partners and allies.

The U.S.'s European Energy Security Policy

Europe is in a unique position with regard to energy security. The region's energy insecurity varies greatly. The nations of Western Europe have traditionally had greater access to diverse supplies of energy resources at competitive prices, particularly natural gas, than their Central and Eastern European counterparts. This is due in part to successful Western European efforts to diversify their sources of supply after Russian gas exports through Ukraine were disrupted in 2006, and once again in 2009. Yet as Western Europe has enjoyed progress, Central and Eastern Europe remain heavily dependent on Russia for their energy supplies, with some

---

[2] W. David Montgomery, Robert Baron, Paul Bernstein, Sugandha D. Tuladhar, Shirley Xiong and Mei Yuan, "Macroeconomic Impacts of LNG Exports from the United States," NERA Economic Consulting, December 2012.

[3] Robert Baron, Paul Bernstein, W. David Montgomery and Sugandha D. Tuladhar, "Updated Macroeconomic Impacts of LNG Exports from the United States," NERA Economic Consulting, February 2014.

[4] "NERA Releases Updated Study on Economic Impacts of LNG Exports," March 6, 2014. http://www.nera.com/83__8451.htm

[5] David L. Goldwyn, "Refreshing European Energy Security Policy: How the U.S. Can Help," Brookings Institution, March 2014 (Goldwyn, 2014)

[6] David L. Goldwyn, "A Modest Proposal for Improving the Department of Energy Non-FTA Liquefied Natural Gas Export Application Process," Brookings Institution, May 2013

[7] The Energy Policy and Conservation Act can be interpreted to require that all agencies responsible for issuing national interest determinations have a responsibility to do so within 90 days after FERC completes its review: "a final decision on a request for a Federal authorization is due no later than 90 days after the Commission issues its final environmental document, unless a schedule is otherwise authorized by Federal law." 18 C.F.R. §157.22

[8] Such a determination would only affect the approval of the export permit application at the Department of Energy, and would not release a company from its environmental assessment requirements before the Federal Energy Regulatory Commission (FERC)

NATO allies, like Bulgaria and Lithuania, wholly dependent on Russian gas. This situation has become starkly clear in the wake of the ongoing events in Crimea.

For many years now, the U.S. has made European energy security a top foreign policy objective. U.S. policy focused on encouraging new suppliers (such as Azerbaijan, Turkmenistan, and Iraq) to send energy to Europe, the promotion of new pipelines and infrastructure, and utilization clean energy technology and energy efficiency. The U.S. has promoted infrastructure projects, like the Baku-Tbilisi-Ceyhan and the Southern Corridor (particularly the Nabucco pipeline), with differing levels of success. We believed a more secure Europe equals a more secure U.S. Independently, Europe has, of course, taken major steps to increase its energy security- approving the Third Energy Package, making destination clauses for natural gas illegal and seeking to create integrated EU markets for electricity and natural gas.

Despite these successes, much of Europe remains energy insecure. In the wake of the crisis in Crimea, energy importing nations were left to wonder whether they would once again suffer as a result of the Russian-Ukrainian dispute, grateful that this crisis did not take place in the depth of winter when another gas shut-off could have been hugely disruptive to their economies. While Western Europe has been able to work to diversify its gas imports through LNG import terminals and agreements with other suppliers, the beneficiaries of geography and relatively strong economies, the nations of Central and Eastern Europe remain dependent on Russia.

To address its energy insecurity Europe will have to make significant strides internally towards further integrating its markets, promoting internal market reform in member countries, developing further infrastructure to support alternative gas supplies and interconnections among member countries, and encouraging indigenous gas development. The U.S. will need to recommit to its Caspian policy, to ensure that the Southern Corridor is completed and that Azerbaijan and Kazakhstan maintain their autonomy and sustain their roles as suppliers of oil and gas to Europe. Refocusing the U.S. policy towards European energy security to consider all of these topics is vital. The U.S. is already active in helping European nations develop their indigenous shale gas resources, through the Global Shale Gas Initiative (GSGI), which I started during my tenure at the U.S. Department of State, now known as the Unconventional Gas Technical Engagement Program (UGTEP), but the U.S. can do more. We can make further integration of European gas markets a key tenet of our engagement in the U.S.-EU Energy Council, and continue to encourage the responsible development of local gas resources. Because the focus of this hearing is U.S. LNG exports, I will limit my remarks on those topics and direct you to the Brookings article submitted to the record for further information.

How Could U.S. LNG Exports Help?

A clear signal from the U.S. that LNG exports will be available to European allies for future purchase would put immediate pressure on Russia's market share, and would also help accelerate investment in and construction of gas transportation infrastructure in Europe. Russia, through its national natural gas company Gazprom, has already found it necessary to renegotiate contracts for natural gas with Western European customers as a result of the U.S. shale gas boom. As many observers have noted, including very recently the Czech Republic's Ambassador-at-Large for Energy Security,[9] the U.S. shale boom resulted in the unexpected availability of LNG cargoes originally destined for the U.S., which increased gas supply to Europe and put downward pressure on prices. Exports of LNG from the U.S. could ensure that the increased negotiating power that Western Europe has had for the past few years is not diminished, and may even be able to extend that negotiating power to the Central and Eastern European nations that remain heavily dependent on Russian exports of natural gas.

A Deloitte report on the international implications of U.S. LNG exports found that even modest levels of U.S. exports, roughly six billion cubic feet per day, would result in wealth transfers from Russia to European consumers of up to four billion dollars, simply as a result of reduced contract prices and lost Russian market share.[10] In terms of European energy security, not to mention economic productivity, that could be considered a success.

Some respected analysts have been too quick to dismiss the connection between U.S. LNG exports and increased European energy security. In dismissing that connection, they make four mistakes: " . . . 1) assuming most U.S. LNG exports will

---

[9] Remarks of Czech Republic Ambassador-at-Large for Energy Security Vaclav Bartuska, Atlantic Council of the United States Conference Call, "Crisis in Ukraine: The Energy Factor," March 17, 2014.

[10] "Exporting the American Renaissance: Global impacts of LNG exports from the United States," Deloitte Center for Energy Solutions and Deloitte MarketPoint, 2013.

go to Asia, 2) assuming the post 2016 delivery time for U.S. LNG will not impact price formation today, 3) underestimating the importance of securing Henry Hub based LNG supply for financing European infrastructure projects and 4) failing to see the immediate strategic importance of degrading Russia's future share of the European gas market."[11]

1) LNG exports to Europe

A number of skeptics have questioned whether Europe would receive any LNG exports from the U.S., arguing that higher priced markets in Asia are more likely to win the cargoes. This view is simplistic. While it is true that gas prices remain higher in Asia than in Europe today, European gas prices remain approximately twice as high as Henry Hub prices. Indeed, European buyers, including Central and Eastern European consumers, have contracts with high-priced suppliers like Russia and Qatar that they are currently seeking to renegotiate. In the event that Russia cuts off supply to Western Europe, European prices could easily approach Asian pricing levels. Asian demand may prove to be weaker than expected in the short to medium term, as a result of nuclear capacity coming back online, and those consumers are also seeking to erode oil-linked pricing. "Meanwhile, the governments of CEE nations are using diplomatic channels to make it clear that they see imports of U.S. gas to be a vital component of their energy diversification strategies.[12] Purchasers weigh price heavily of course, but they also weigh the diversity of supply source, and the likelihood of timely project completion."[13,14]

2) Price Formation

As stated previously, long-term gas supply prices are formed based on future price and supply expectations. Energy is a business where the marginal barrel (or cargo) sets the price, and the lead times for project development can be long. Every decision, from investments in oil and gas to production to power generation infrastructure to the construction of LNG import or export terminals, is based on future price expectations. Allowing US based LNG to compete for market share in Europe could decrease Russia's future market share in Europe, and ensure that the gas that they do provide is competitively priced. The availability of alternative supply is central to the continent's energy security, and the availability of American LNG supplies may be the only direct tool that the U.S. has to achieve that goal.

3) Financing New Infrastructure

It is true that commercial parties, rather than governments, make final investment decisions about infrastructure development in Western nations. However, commercial energy infrastructure projects are difficult to develop without access to reliable, competitively priced sources of supply. The availability of U.S. LNG supply at prices that are competitive against piped Russian gas or oil-linked Qatar gas will make it easier to develop much-needed infrastructure projects in Europe.

4) Degrading Russia's Market Share

Disregarding the benefits of U.S. LNG exports simply because they won't be available until 2016 or beyond is short sighted, at best. Energy consumers are looking for natural gas supplies to purchase in the future, because they have generally already contracted long-term supply through 2016 or so. The U.S. policy regarding European energy security has been predicated on the pursuit of long-term projects that would ensure supply diversity. The Southern Corridor will not be in place till 2018. Potential supplies from East Africa will not enter the market until after 2020. Our litmus test (and time horizon) for assisting European consumers dependent on Russian gas supply should be forward-looking, extending far beyond how we help them next week.

---

[11] Goldwyn, 2014

[12] Multiple nations have been vocal about their desire to import U.S. LNG. The Ambassadors of the Visegrad 4 nations (Poland, the Czech Republic, Hungary and Slovakia) sent a letter to Congressional Leadership asking them to remove the bureaucratic hurdles surrounding export permits; meanwhile plans are in the works to create a lobbying group named "LNG Allies," which will represent a larger group of countries and lobby the U.S. government in favor of LNG exports. (Amy Harder, "Europe to America: We Want Your Gas," National Journal, January 16, 2014; Veronika Gulyas, "Central Europe Turns to U.S. for Natural Gas," Wall Street Journal, March 10, 2014)

[13] While LNG projects are being developed globally, many of the projects abroad have suffered from major delays and cost overruns, including some of the large-scale projects under development in Australia and the South Pacific. (Ed Crooks, "Cost of Australia's Gorgon LNG project rises to $54bn," Financial Times, December 12, 2013)

[14] Goldwyn, 2014

The LNG Approval Process: A Source of Uncertainty

Today, companies seeking to export LNG from the U.S. are required to seek a national interest determination from the U.S. Department of Energy. Applications to export LNG to countries that the U.S. has free trade agreements (FTA) with are automatically determined to be in the national interest, in accordance with Section 3 of the Natural Gas Act.[15] Applications for exports to non-FTA nations, on the other hand, go through a longer national interest determination process, in which the Department of Energy considers the applications on a case-by-case basis, assessing the cumulative impacts of LNG exports. The uncertainty that results from this process is a result of the opaqueness of the process and there is no clear timeline for the approval or denial of projects. This uncertainty makes it difficult for potential suppliers of U.S. LNG to secure financing for their projects and for consumers abroad to accurately assess and compare potential suppliers when they seek to sign contracts.

The U.S. could minimize this uncertainty by deeming exports of natural gas to be in the national interest, regardless of whether their destination is to FTA or non-FTA nations. This would allow the market to decide whether supplies will go to Europe or Asia. While this might be the economically optimal approach, it has obvious political challenges and the Department of Energy has other choices. One would be to grant early preference to the countries of Central and Eastern Europe and Japan, which would allow projects with those customers to enjoy a financing advantage and accelerated consideration. This will help countries most in need but picks winners in a way that could invite trade based challenges. A process-based improvement would be to allow commercially mature projects (those with contracts and which have obtained FERC environmental clearance) to be considered promptly by DOE, either by jumping to the head of the queue or by agreeing to consider them within 90 days of obtaining FERC approval. There are multiple options available; the U.S. should choose an option that will signal certainty that U.S.-based LNG can be available to the market sooner rather than later. These regulations were developed in an era where today's abundance of natural gas could not be predicted or expected, and, as a result, bear reconsideration.

The Impact on Asia

Removing uncertainty from the LNG permitting process would also benefit Asian consumers, and assist the U.S. as it refocuses a larger share of diplomatic attention to Asian partners and allies. Natural gas consumers in Asia pay extraordinarily high prices to secure LNG supplies, and are actively seeking new supplies abroad. As U.S. natural gas prices hover around $4.50/mmBtu, Asian LNG benchmarks have at times exceeded $20.00/mmBtu this year.[16] Henry Hub-linked U.S. LNG contracts should thus prove highly competitive in Asia even when one factors in liquefaction, transportation, and regasification costs, which are widely anticipated to be around $6-$8/mmBtu. Henry Hub-linked contracts will provide Asian buyers, including U.S. allies and top global LNG importers South Korea and Japan, with increased negotiating leverage and pricing flexibility. This may prove especially crucial to Japan, which is suffering from record trade deficits stemming from increased LNG purchases following the 2011 Fukushima Daiichi nuclear disaster.

Other nations are also seeking to develop LNG export capabilities, some of them closer to Asia geographically. Yet many of these projects have been plagued by unanticipated cost overruns, while others are located in areas where scarce infrastructure and government corruption and rent seeking threaten to delay export timetables. Consumers in Asia have the same commercial concerns as consumers elsewhere in the world, and they value competitive costs, reliability and timeliness. The U.S. is known worldwide as a reliable trading partner, and it can play that role for Asia as well. Exports of LNG to Asia would be in the U.S.'s economic and strategic interests. Given recent events, it is worth mentioning that Russia aspires to double its share of the global LNG trade by 2020 in large part by meeting large shares of Asian demand growth. Russia is seeking closer relationships with Asian consumers like Japan and is negotiating a gas pipeline deal with China that would provide almost 40 bcm per year to China for 30 years and cost roughly $50 billion[17]—but not until after 2018. We need to ask ourselves if we would prefer for Asia to plan to rely on Russian gas or on U.S. LNG as it builds its strategic alliances. As in Europe, U.S. LNG exports may one of the few direct tools the U.S. possesses to

---

[15] 15 USC §717b

[16] Eric Yep, "Spot LNG Prices Hit Record in Asia," Wall Street Journal, February 14, 2013

[17] Jack Farchy, "Russia looks to sell energy beyond Europe," Financial Times, March 20, 2014

limit Russian market share and better ensure the Russian gas that is exported to Asia is done so at competitive prices.

Conclusion

U.S. LNG exports, while no panacea, provide the U.S. with a strategic advantage for achieving greater global energy security and greater stability in natural gas markets. My colleagues at Brookings concluded in 2012 that the optimal policy regarding LNG exports from the U.S. would be to allow the market to decide where exports should go and at what volume, without promoting or restricting them.[18] I share that view, and believe that significantly speeding up the national interest determination process at the Department of Energy would allow the market to work more efficiently. Unfortunately, that optimal policy arrangement is unavailable to us today.

As General Martin Dempsey, Chairman of the Joint Chiefs of Staff, observed in a House Committee on Appropriations hearing less than two weeks ago, "an energy-independent and net-exporter of energy as a nation [sic] has the potential to change the security environment around the world, notably in Europe and in the Middle East. And so, as we look at our strategies for the future, I think we've got to pay more and particular attention to energy as an instrument of national power."[19] A number of influential observers in Washington and beyond, from both sides of the partisan aisle, concur that LNG exports are in the interest of the U.S., and have weighed in in favor of exports as a tool for reducing Russia's dominance in European energy markets. Several pieces of bipartisan legislation have been introduced in both Chambers of the Congress that would authorize exports of U.S. LNG to our allies, be they NATO or WTO members.

The geopolitical imperative is clear. The Russian dominance of European energy markets and the predominance of high-cost oil-linked gas prices in both Europe and Asia threaten the energy security of our friends and allies, and of the U.S. by extension. In an increasingly globalized world, an insular policy regarding LNG exports is not in the interest of the U.S. The U.S. consistently supports opening markets throughout the world to create new opportunities and shared prosperity with our allies and partners. Our broader policies and goals are at odds with current restrictions on both LNG and crude oil exports, and this inconsistency does not go unnoticed by negotiating partners. These policies, which were developed during an era of energy scarcity, merit reconsideration given our current energy abundance. In the absence of the optimal policy arrangement, in which LNG exports would be free to flow as directed by the market, we should consider unfettering LNG exports to our friends and allies in Europe as a first step.

I close today as I closed my article for Brookings:

> We have spent nearly two decades of intense diplomacy trying to diversify Europe's energy supply by getting Azerbaijan, Kazakhstan, Turkmenistan and even Iraq to sell them energy. Baku-Tbilisi-Ceyhan. Nabucco. The Southern Corridor. The Trans-Caspian Gas Pipeline. We finally have a tool at our disposal that can provide direct relief to Europe over time, and accelerate the competitiveness of that market today. We want everyone else to help. Shouldn't we?[20]

The CHAIR. Thank you very much.

Mr. Chow.

STATEMENT OF EDWARD C. CHOW, SENIOR FELLOW, ENERGY AND NATIONAL SECURITY PROGRAM, CENTER FOR STRATEGIC AND INTERNATIONAL STUDIES (CSIS)

Mr. CHOW. Madame Chair, members of the committee, it is my honor to appear before you today to discuss the important questions you have posed.

First of all, let me congratulate you, Senator Landrieu, for chairing what I understand to be, your first full committee hearing and also for being on the Kremlin's sanctioned list.

[Laughter.]

---

[18] Ebinger, 2012

[19] "A Gas Export Strategy: Opponents don't understand energy markets or price expectations." Wall Street Journal, March 19, 2014.

[20] Goldwyn, 2014

Mr. CHOW. You must the envy of your colleagues in more ways than one.

I understand the committee would like me to focus on the international impact of the unconventional oil and gas revolution, particularly in light of the current crises over Russia's invasion of Ukraine's territory of Crimea and the potential threat it poses for gas supply disruptions for Ukraine as well as for Europe. Of course the long term impact of the unconventional revolution is just beginning to be felt internationally. Much depends on whether the American experience can be replicated around the world.

Studies indicate shale plays exist in different parts of the world. The history of technology makes me optimistic that this advancement will be transferred to other countries. It would just take time as the application of new technology is adapted to local conditions.

Even before spreading to other countries the tight oil and shale gas revolution has already made important contributions to the stability of global markets. Thanks to tight oil U.S. oil production increased by more than 2 million barrels per day since 2010 partially offsetting global supply disruptions in recent years. American shale gas already had significant impact on the global LNG market even before the start of exports.

As you pointed out, Madame Chair, more than 30 regassification terminals were proposed in the U.S. for imports, not exports, at one time. Imagine what the international LNG market would be like if the U.S. had become a major importer rather than expected to become a net gas exporter by 2018. U.S. LNG exports could lead to important changes to the global gas market.

Because we have gas on gas competition in North America natural gas prices are not linked to oil prices as they are in most of the rest of the world when gas is traded internationally. Our exports will also contribute to increased spot LNG cargoes that are not tied to long term contracts.

When the first project for exporting LNG from the lower 48 States is completed Sabine Pass, which I'm sure Madame Chair, you are very familiar with, will have taken more than 5 years to complete. It is not merely governmental approval such as those from DOE or FERC and local permitting that takes time, but also negotiating purchase agreements with qualified buyers, securing financing and the standard engineering procurement and construction work to build the export terminal.

The combined capacity of the projects DOE has already conditionally approved is higher than the total gas consumption of Germany. The U.S. will become a major LNG exporter if all the projects are completed. More export projects are in the queue for DOE approval.

There are ample domestic economic reasons why restrictions on oil and gas exports should be relaxed. With oil, the light, sweet crude being produced from shale plays, like the Bakken, cannot be run optimally by our sophisticated refineries which are designed to process less expensive, heavier, sour crudes. We would maximize the economic benefits of tight oil production by exporting some light, sweet crudes and condensate while continuing to import heavier and sour crudes.

With gas, exports would help to sustain the level of investment in production when priced with price levels that benefit both producers and long term consumers without depressed prices choking off the expected growth. These are complicated issues that deserve full debate in Congress as has already begun. Decades of perceived energy scarcity informed our existing oil and gas export policies and it takes time to reexamine these policies and amend applicable law in a new era of energy abundance.

A degree of regulatory certainty is important when billions of dollars are at stake in investments that take years to complete. Russian aggression against Ukraine has added geopolitical and foreign policy dimensions to these issues. Some argue that hastening approvals of crude oil and LNG exports by the United States would have a deterrent effect on hostile actions by Russia. Unfortunately this is unlikely to have much immediate effect.

Russia produces more than 10 million barrels per day of oil and exports about 7 million barrels in crude and petroleum products. No amount of increases in U.S. exports can begin to replace such large volumes. Russian exports of natural gas are more than twice the combined capacity of DOE approved U.S. LNG export projects so far.

In order to reduce the influence Russia exerts through oil and gas Europe plays the crucial role as Russia is more dependent on Europe as the destination of its exports than Europe is reliant on Russia for supply. Europe would do well to focus on developing indigenous energy resources in order to be less import dependent and fully integrating its gas and electricity networks so that supply can flow more easily to countries vulnerable to cutoffs. Unfortunately Lithuania, where the Minister is from, is one of the few European countries committed to developing shale gas.

Export of U.S. LNG is not a silver bullet for Europe. In fact, LNG imports declined significantly in Europe last year as a result of more favorable pricing terms authored by traditional pipeline suppliers such as Norway and Russia. Unlike countries such as Russia, the United States does not direct commerce and leave it to private companies to operate freely in the market, except in times of war and other national emergency. Indeed we have historically taken a stance against the use of energy as the geopolitical weapon, especially after the Arab oil embargo of 1973.

Inflating the rhetoric on exports could actually embolden Russia since it recognizes it's irrelevant and a short run. More importantly, it can distract us from the critical task of shoring Ukraine economically.

I know the committee may have more questions on Ukraine. It is a country I've spent some time working in. I will wait until the question and answer period to address those.

[The prepared statement of Mr. Chow follows:]

STATEMENT OF EDWARD C. CHOW, SENIOR FELLOW, ENERGY AND NATIONAL SECURITY PROGRAM, CENTER FOR STRATEGIC AND INTERNATIONAL STUDIES (CSIS)

INTERNATIONAL IMPACT OF THE U.S. UNCONVENTIONAL OIL AND GAS REVOLUTION

Madam Chair, Members of the Committee: It is my honor to appear before your Committee today to discuss the important questions you have posed.

My fellow panelists have already described very well the significant impact of the shale gas and tight oil revolution and the long lasting effects on America's energy supply. Indeed this is the most important development in energy production in the 21st Century so far, driven in part by the equally phenomenal increases in oil prices since the beginning of the century.

I understand the Committee would like me to focus on the international impact of the unconventional oil and gas revolution, particularly in light of the current crisis over Russia's invasion of Ukraine's territory of Crimea and the potential threat it poses for gas supply disruptions for Ukraine as well as for Europe, and the possibility for U.S. oil and gas exports to enhance global energy security.

Of course, the international impact of unconventional revolution in North America is just beginning to be felt. Much depends on whether the North American experience can be replicated around the world and how quickly the new technology can be introduced in countries with significant unconventional resource potential like China and Argentina. Numerous studies, including those commissioned by the Energy Information Administration of the Department of Energy (DOE), suggest that similar shale plays exist in different parts of the world. However, even if the geology is similar, the above-ground conditions in most of the world are so different from those in the U.S. that it will take some time, at least another three to five years, before we can know whether and how the American success can be repeated in other countries.

These non-geological conditions, which are somewhat unique for the U.S., include private landholders' ownership of subsurface mineral rights, a geological data base from a century and half of oil and gas production, a robust and competitive oil and gas industry (especially the presence of small to medium-size, nimble and innovative producers, equipment suppliers, and service companies), existing infrastructure to transport and process production, liberalized market pricing, and well-established and a transparent regulatory environment, which took decades to develop.

Most of these conditions do not exist elsewhere in the world. However, the history of technology transfer makes me optimistic that this technological advancement will be introduced successfully in other countries. It will just take time as it did for our country and longer than some of its eager champions would like. The way it will be implemented may also differ from how it is done in the U.S., but it will be adapted to local conditions.

Nevertheless, tight oil and shale gas developments in the U.S. have already made important contributions to the stability of global energy markets. Thanks to tight oil, U.S. oil production increased by more than two million barrels per day since 2010. This is a remarkable achievement. Without this additional supply, it is difficult to imagine how global oil prices could have remained around $100 per barrel. Supply disruptions from Libya, Sudan and Iran, as well as underperformance in production in Iraq, Nigeria, and Venezuela were partially offset by the greatest volume increase in the history of oil production in the U.S.

Even before we start exporting liquefied natural gas (LNG) from the lower 48 states, the American shale gas revolution has already made a significant impact on the global LNG market. As recently as 2004, more than 30 LNG regasification terminals were proposed in the U.S. for imports, not exports. The long-term impact of natural gas deregulation under President Carter in 1978 allowed market clearing pricing, unshackled by state and federal controls, to encourage conservation and domestic production. Thirty-five years of stable and predictable regulatory regimes created investment conditions for energy efficiency improvements and innovation in production, such as hydraulic fracturing. Of the 30 some LNG import terminals proposed, only five were actually completed and became operational.

What would the global LNG market be like if the U.S. had become a major LNG importer rather than expected to become a net gas exporter by 2018? LNG from Qatar, West Africa, Trinidad/Tobago and elsewhere, slated for the U.S. market, all became available for Europe and, more importantly, to satisfy increased needs from Japan after the Fukushima disaster and rising import demand by China and India.

When U.S. LNG exports begin by 2016, in addition to adding more global supply, they may also lead to evolution of the global gas market. Because we have gas-on-gas competition in North America, natural gas prices are not linked to oil prices as they are in the rest of the world when gas is traded internationally. The U.S. will become a net gas exporter before the end of this decade. Higher LNG volumes globally, including those from increased production from Australia, potential new production from East Africa, Russia and the Eastern Mediterranean, may contribute to increased spot LNG cargoes that are not tied to long-term contracts with strict volume commitments by both buyers and sellers.

In time, the LNG market may look more like the more liquid and flexible international oil market. However, this will take some time to develop, particularly since the new liquefaction projects are high-cost, demanding tens of billions of dollars in investment, which will continue to require long-term contracts from committed, creditworthy buyers and predictable gas pricing or tolling charges in order to secure financing.

An indication of the radical change the shale gas revolution caused in the U.S. is Cheniere Energy's Sabine Pass LNG project. Sabine Pass was completed as a receiving terminal only in 2009 and almost immediately sought to become a bi-directional terminal that can liquefy and export gas as well. It will become the first LNG export terminal in the lower 48 states when it is completed by yearend 2015, a journey of more than five years from conception to completion, which is quick for a multi-billion project in the oil and gas industry. It is not merely governmental approvals, such as those from DOE or the Federal Energy Regulatory Commission (FERC) and local permitting, that take time, but also negotiating purchase agreements with qualified buyers, securing financing, and the standard engineering, procurement, and construction work to build the export terminal.

So far, DOE has granted conditional approvals to six LNG liquefaction and export projects. (Sabine Pass is the only one that also has FERC approval.) The last project, Jordan Cove, received its approval only yesterday morning. In fact, DOE has been remarkably speedy in granting such conditional approvals in the last year or so, as confidence grew on the resource base estimates and recovery rates for shale gas.

The combined capacity of the six projects (9.3 bcf/day or 95 bcma) is higher than the total gas consumption of Germany. The U.S. will truly become a major LNG exporter if all six projects are completed. Another twenty-four export projects are in the queue for DOE approval. Consequently, the potential impact on the global gas market could be even greater. Of course, just because a project is proposed does not mean it will be built, as we discovered with the 30-some LNG receiving terminal proposed not too long ago.

There are ample domestic economic reasons why restrictions on oil and gas exports should be relaxed. With oil, the light sweet crude being produced from shale plays like the Bakken cannot be optimally utilized by our sophisticated refineries, which are configured to process less-expensive heavier sour crudes. The U.S. would maximize the economic benefits of tight oil production by exporting some domestically produced light sweet crudes and condensate while continuing to import heavier and sour grades.

With gas, exports would help to sustain the level of investment in production with market prices that benefit producers and long-term consumers without depressed pricing choking off the expected growth, as has happened in the past. This includes gas consumers who are considering expansion of petrochemical capacity, increased utilization in power generation, and new uses for gas such as in the transportation sector.

These are complicated issues that deserve full debate in Congress, as has already begun. Ever since the end of World War II, the U.S. has championed free trade around the world and its benefits extend equally to oil and gas trade. However, decades of perceived energy scarcity have informed our existing oil and gas export policies and it will take time to reexamine these policies and amend applicable laws for a period of relative domestic energy abundance. A degree of certainty in investment climate is important when billions of dollars are at stake in projects that take years to complete in order to produce, process, and consume more domestic oil and gas.

Russia's aggression against Ukraine has added a geopolitical and foreign policy dimension to these questions. Some have argued that hastening U.S. approvals of crude oil and LNG exports would have a deterrent effect on further Russian actions and enhance the energy supply security of our allies and trading partners in Europe. Unfortunately, this is unlikely to have much immediate effect.

Russia produces more than 10 million barrels of oil per day and exports about 7 million barrels in crude and petroleum products. No amount of increases in U.S. oil exports, including possible drawdown from the Strategic Petroleum Reserve (at a maximum rate of 4 million barrels per day for 90 days), can replace such large volumes. Russian exports of natural gas are equivalent to twice the combined capacity of the seven DOE-approved U.S. LNG export projects, which may be completed by the end of this decade. Certainly increased exports of oil and gas from the U.S. and other countries would reduce over time the significance of Russian exports, but none of this will happen quickly.

In order to reduce the influence Russia exerts through its oil and gas exports, it is Europe's role that is crucial. Whereas it is true that Europe relies on Russia as its major oil and gas supplier, Russia is even more reliant on the European market as the destination of 80 percent of its oil and gas exports. Oil and gas represent more than 70 percent of Russia's export earnings and more than 50 percent of its federal budget. So, who is more reliant on whom? This has more to do with the exercise of political will rather than of economic leverage.

Europe would do well to focus on the development of indigenous energy resources, including shale gas through hydraulic fracturing (unfortunately the Lithuanian Minister's country is one of the few which has committed to do so), and to fully integrating its gas and electricity networks so that supply can flow more easily to countries vulnerable to cutoffs.

Export of U.S. LNG is not a silver bullet for Europe. In fact, imports of LNG declined significantly in Europe last year as a result of more favorable pricing terms offered by traditional pipeline suppliers such as Norway and Russia, and as an indirect result of American shale gas reducing our imports. Operators of European LNG terminals are hurting financially because of low utilization rates. The future volumes of U.S. LNG are already contractually committed to buyers, mostly in Asia where LNG prices are significantly higher than Europe's. Of course, some of these volumes could be redirected if Europe is willing to pay equally high prices for LNG.

Unlike countries such as Russia that have oil and gas sectors dominated by state-owned and controlled companies, the U.S. Government does not direct commerce and leaves this to private companies operating in a free market, except in times of war and other national emergency. Indeed we have historically taken a stance against the use of energy as a geopolitical weapon, especially after the Arab oil embargo of 1973. These are principles worth considering before we decide to select politically the countries with which we trade oil and gas rather than through internationally negotiated trade agreements.

Since U.S. exports of oil and natural gas would have no impact on Russia's market position in the short to medium term, there is a danger that inflating the rhetoric on exports would actually embolden Russia, which will recognize this as an empty threat, to act even more recklessly. It can also distract us from the more critical task of shoring up Ukraine economically. Two years ago, I testified before the Europe Subcommittee of the Senate Foreign Relations Committee to warn that for more than twenty years "Ukraine has been on a dangerous path toward energy insecurity, which has accelerated" under the Yanukovych administration and that at this rate "Ukraine (will) become an energy appendage of Russia's."

The situation has only worsened in the intervening two years. Ukraine is truly vulnerable to energy blackmail by Russia because of past leaders, not just Yanukovych, who personally benefited from pervasive corruption in the sector, especially in the gas trade with Russia, that led to wasteful consumption, depressed domestic production, and fed the overreliance on Russia for energy supplies. Ukraine is one of the most natural gas dependent countries in the world, with gas supplying 40 percent of primary energy, 60 percent of which is imported from Russia. Potential economic collapse presents the greatest long-term threat to Ukraine's national unity and its territorial integrity beyond Crimea.

Reverse flows of pipelines from Central and Eastern Europe can supply, at most, less than half of the gas Ukraine currently imports from Russia. They are also worthless in a true supply cutoff by Russia lasting for more than a few weeks, since countries like Poland, Slovakia, Hungary and Romania will then have no gas to spare for export to Ukraine. Ukraine has no LNG receiving terminal and, even if it had the wherewithal to build one, which it does not, it would take at least two years to put a receiving facility in place.

Fortunately more than half of the Russian gas sold to Europe still transits Ukraine and Russia cannot cut off Ukraine without cutting off its European customers, upon whom it depends for revenue (as we learned from the 2006 and 2009 gas crisis). Therefore, unless the security and political situation deteriorates further between the two countries, neither Russia nor Ukraine would precipitate a gas supply cutoff. Unfortunately, the risks have increased in recent days.

Nevertheless, urgent actions are needed to remedy Ukraine's long-term gas supply vulnerability, which also affects Europe. Fortunately, the solutions are well known since Ukrainian and Western experts have recommended sensible reform steps for many years, including two separate studies by the International Energy Agency, most recently in 2012. Almost all of these reform plans were commissioned by the same Ukrainian governments that lacked the political will to implement them.

Especially important is gas price decontrol at the burner tip, as the IMF insists for fiscal and balance of payments reasons, but also at the wellhead to provide incentives to invest in domestic production. Current gas price regulations encourage wasteful consumption and chronic shortage, as well as depress domestic production since domestic gas price is controlled at a small fraction of imported gas price. This also has the intended effect of facilitating widespread corruption in gas trade. This must stop.

All Western financial aid to Ukraine from the U.S., E.U., and international financial institutions (IMF, World Bank, EBRD, EIB) should be conditional on the agreement by the interim government of Ukraine to international monitoring of fundamental reforms of the energy sector and a sufficient share of the Western aid money devoted to funding the implementation of reforms, especially in gas pricing, in order to improve energy efficiency and promote domestic production. Naftogaz, the state oil and gas monopoly, which is at the center of energy corruption in Ukraine, must be completely restructured as soon as possible.

There is no point pretending with the new authorities in Kyiv that there are solutions, absent fundamental reform, to Ukraine's energy supply vulnerability, which hangs like a Sword of Damocles over it and Europe because of Ukraine's central position in energy transit. If the Ukrainian government commits to such reforms, the U.S. and E.U. must assist in capacity building for proper execution of reforms steps by providing teams of technical, financial, business and regulatory experts to help.

Frankly, $1 billion in loan guarantees is not sufficient to the challenge at hand if the U.S. is serious about helping Ukraine's long-delayed transition into a market economy, including modernizing its energy sector. Ukraine's long-suffering public also has to be prepared for the short-term pain energy reform will bring in order to reap its long-term benefits. This will not be easy.

Ukraine's geological endowment for producing more oil and gas is well known. The fastest way of tapping into this potential is to revive its conventional oil and gas production, which has stagnated for more than twenty years in spite of high imported prices, by deregulating wellhead prices as the U.S. did more than thirty years ago. With liberalized pricing, Ukraine may even lead the rest of Europe in replicating American success in shale gas, as it appears similarly well endowed in potential shale plays and major international oil companies seem interested to invest under the right conditions. That would be the best and most realistic way for America's unconventional oil and gas revolution to contribute to the future of European energy security.

The CHAIR. Thank you very much. An interesting perspective.

We now will hear from the Minister of Lithuania, the Honorable Jaroslav Neverovi.

STATEMENT OF JAROSLAV NEVEROVIČ, MINISTRY OF ENERGY, THE REPUBLIC OF LITHUANIA

Mr. NEVEROVIČ. Thank you, Madame Chair, members of the committee, thank you very much for making——

The CHAIR. Speak into your mic. You have to lean in. It's a little awkward, sorry.

Mr. NEVEROVIČ. Yes.

Thank you very much for making me a part of this hearing. I will share with you Lithuania's story which I can summarize with one phrase and which is, "Freedom is not for free."

But before I make my point I want to return to May 8th, 2003 when the historic vote happened on the Senate Floor on enlargement of NATO. One year later we became formal members of NATO. This year we celebrate tenth anniversary of our membership. Senators, Senate's role could not be underestimated. So thank you very much for your leadership then.

During the past quarter of a century Lithuania emerged from the ruined Soviet economy to become a free market Nation with a robust economy, stable political system. We have become a trusted international partner. We are cooperating closely with the United States including fighting terrorism in places such as Afghanistan. We are very proud of our achievements.

I'm honored to appear here before a such distinguished group of American officials led by chairwoman of this committee, Senator Mary Landrieu, the respective of political affiliation you individually and collectively stand proudly for the principles of free and fair trade and understand implicitly that unrestricted flow of good services and energy resources benefits both the United States and your trading partners.

Madame chairwoman and committee members we have common vision for democratic system which are same values in international relations. But despite our unwavering commitment to those principles and ideals a law enacted in your country some 75 years ago denies us access to your abundant energy resources. Let's change that situation in the spirit of allies, let the energy strengthen and deepen our strategic cooperation.

At present we are completely 100 percent dependent upon single supplier of natural gas. As a result are forced to pay a political price for this vital energy resource. Lithuanian families and businesses pay 30 percent more for natural gas than citizens in other European countries. This is not fair. That's abuse of monopoly position.

I'm here today to tell you that Lithuania is taking steps to achieve energy independence and thereby strengthen our national security. But let me also be 100 percent transparent. I am also here to plead with you and your colleagues to do everything within your power to expedite the release of some of your abundant natural gas resources into the world market, especially to those Nations beholden to monopolistic supplier. The United States, with your enormous natural gas resources and highly developed infrastructure, has the kind of liquid market that Europe is trying to build right now.

So what is the potential in Europe to receive U.S. LNG?

There are currently 22 operating LNG import facilities within the EU with total combined capacity of 6.7 trillion cubic feet per year and another 6 terminals with additional capacity of over one trillion cubic feet per year under construction. However, the actual import of LNG into Europe fell about almost half between 2010 and last year. Because LNG prices are generally pegged to the global price of oil, current prices are just too high to supplant natural gas produced in Russia and elsewhere on the continent.

As a consequence LNG terminals across Europe are functioning near their minimum technical capacities.

However, America's entry into the global natural gas market can change this situation completely. Last week Vice President Biden visited Vilnius, Lithuania. During his visit the Vice President said, "We have learned the hard way that protecting the sovereignty of Nations depends on having more than one supplier of energy." Vice President Biden expressed support to our efforts by encouragement for further energy cooperation.

Indeed Baltic States are working successfully to overcome "energy island" situation.

I'm pleased to tell you that in just 250 more days Lithuania will have an instrument, our own LNG import terminal in our seaport, Klaip.da. The newly built, floating storage and regassification vessel has been symbolically named, "Independence." Also its primary goal is to satisfy our national needs, the terminal will operate under so-called third party access regime. That means that our neighboring countries could use terminal's capacity to meet their own needs. Thus our terminal, the first, large scale LNG import facility on the Baltic Sea will be the ice breaker for the region, helping to ensure alternative gas supply.

While the United States appears positioned to be a key player in the global LNG marketplace there is, as you know, a sticking point. The majority of your LNG exports are subject to a public interest review. We understand that the U.S. President has the authority to deem all of the pending applications to export LNG to non-FTA Nations to be in public interest. We hope that this Administration will do just that by opening the doors to LNG exports to non-FTA countries.

But if they don't act in a timely way we urge Congress to step in and amend the law. Accelerating America's entry into the global natural gas market is a win/win/win situation.

America wins through job creation, economic growth, more avenues for the government.

Customers in Europe win by access to more competitively priced gas from U.S.

Strategic operation of NATO allies would be strengthened.

Consequently stability on the European continent wins when monopolistic levers of influence are reduced or eliminated.

The present situation in Ukraine has taught us one lesson. No Nation should be able to use its monopolistic energy supplies to punish any other Nation.

So in conclusion, we should work together to let competition in, to keep the monopoly out and to bring natural gas prices down for customers in America and in Europe.

Thank you.

[The prepared statement of Mr. Neverovič follows:]

PREPARED STATEMENT OF JAROSLAV NEVEROVIČ, MINISTER OF ENERGY, THE REPUBLIC OF LITHUANIA

Madam Chairwoman and members of the committee. Thank you for the opportunity to appear before you this morning to tell Lithuania's story, which I would summarize in a simple phrase: Freedom Isn't Free!

Just eleven years ago-on May 8, 2003-the historic vote of the Senate occurred, unanimously ratifying the accession of Lithuania and six other European democracies to NATO. As a result during these days we are celebrating the 10th anniversary of our membership at the Alliance.

During the past quarter century, Lithuania emerged from the ruined Soviet economy to become a free market nation with a robust economy, stable political system. We've become a trusted international partner, we are cooperating closely with the United States. We've put our own soldiers shoulder-to-shoulder with yours to fight terrorism in places such as Afghanistan. And, we're very proud of that.

So, I am humbled and honored to be here today as the energy minister of the free and independent state of Lithuania!

I am also honored to appear here because this body-the United States Senate-always stood beside us, never once recognizing the illegal and immoral annexation of the Baltic States by the Soviet Union.

And, finally, I am honored to appear before such a distinguished group of American officials, led by the chairwoman of this committee, Senator Mary Landrieu from the great state of Louisiana. Irrespective of political affiliation, you individually and collectively stand proudly for the principles of free and fair trade and understand implicitly that the unrestricted flow of goods, services, and energy resources benefits both the United States and your trading partners.

Madam Chairwoman and committee members, the Lithuanian message is simple. We have common democratic vision; we share the same values in international relations. But, despite our unwavering commitment to those principles and ideals, a law enacted in your country some 75 years ago denies us access to your abundant and affordably priced energy resources.

Let's change this strange situation. In the spirit of allies let the energy strengthen and deepen our strategic cooperation.

At present, we are completely-100 percent-dependent upon single supplier of natural gas and, as a result, are forced to pay a political price for this vital energy resource. Lithuanian families and businesses pay 30 percent more for natural gas than citizens in other European countries. This is not just unfair. This is abuse of monopolist position.

Madam Chairwoman and committee members, I am here today to tell you about the steps Lithuania is taking to achieve energy independence and thereby strengthen our national security. But, let me also be 100 percent transparent. I am also here to plead with you and your colleagues to do everything within your power to help us achieve that objective by expediting the release of some of your abundant natural gas resources into the world market, especially to those nations beholden to a monopolistic supplier.

The United States, with your enormous natural gas resources and highly developed infrastructure, has the kind of liquid market that Europe is trying mightily to achieve.

What is the potential in Europe to receive US LNG? There are currently 22 operating LNG import facilities within the EU with a total combined capacity of 6,7 trillion cubic feet (Tcf) per year and another six terminals with an additional capacity of 1,06 trillion cubic feet per year are under construction (one of those new facilities, as I shall explain, is located in Lithuania's Port of Klaipeda on the Baltic Sea).

However, the actual import of LNG into Europe fell by almost half between 2010 and 2013, from 3 trillion cubic feet per year to 1,6 Tcf per year. The reason for this decline is simple. Because LNG prices are generally pegged to the global price of oil, current prices are just too high to supplant natural gas produced in Russia and elsewhere on the continent. As a consequence, LNG terminal across Europe are functioning near their minimum technical capacities.

However, America's entry into the global natural gas market can change this situation completely.

Last week Vice President Biden visited Lithuania. During his visit, the Vice President said: "We have learned the hard way that protecting the sovereignty of nations depends on having more than one supplier of energy". Vice President Biden expressed support to our efforts by encouragement for further energy cooperation.

Lack of gas and electricity interconnections with other EU members and extremely high dependency on energy from a single monopolistic supplier, makes us highly vulnerable. Fortunately, the Baltic States are working successfully to overcome this "energy island" situation.

I am pleased to tell you that in just 250 more days, Lithuania will have an instrument-our own LNG import terminal in our seaport Klaipeda-and once this facility is operational, we will have a functional natural gas market at last.

I cannot overstress the strategic importance of the LNG terminal to Lithuania. The newly-built floating storage and regasification vessel has been symbolically named "Independence" and although its primary goal is to satisfy our national needs, the terminal will operate under a so-called "third party access" regime. That means that our neighboring countries could use terminal's capacity to meet their own needs. Thus our terminal-the first large-scale LNG import facility on the Baltic Sea-will be the ice-breaker for the region, helping to ensure an alternative gas supply and create a functioning gas market.

While the United States appears positioned to be a key player in the global LNG marketplace, there is, as you know, a sticking point. The majority of your LNG exports are subject to a "public interest" review conducted by your Department of Energy. At present, only exports destined for nations with which you have a free trade agreement are automatically deemed to be "in the public interest."

However, the U.S. President has the authority to deem all of the pending applications to export LNG to non-FTA nations to be "in the public interest". We hope that his administration will do just that by opening the doors to LNG export to non-FTA NATO members. But, if they don't act in a timely way, we urge Congress to step in and amend the law.

Accelerating America's entry into the global natural gas market is a win-win-win situation. America wins through job creation, economic growth, more revenues for government. Customers across Europe win by access to more competitive, clean-burning U.S. natural gas. And, strategic cooperation of NATO allies would be strengthened-consequently stability on the European continent wins when monopolistic levers of influence are reduced or eliminated.

The present situation in Ukraine has taught us all one lesson-no nation should be able to use its monopolistic energy supplies to punish any other nation. So, in conclusion, my message to you is simple. Let's work together to let competition in, push the monopolists out, and bring natural gas prices down in Europe as they have come down in America.

Thank you for the opportunity to make this statement. I look forward to your questions.

The CHAIR. Thank you very much.

We'll begin with a round of questioning.

Senator Murkowski, welcome. She's going to forego her opening statement on the matter, for the matter of time. But will join me in an opening round of questions.

Then the order will be Senator Wyden, Senator Scott, Senator Udall and then I'll come back to the list.

Thank you all for being present.

Let me ask this first, I think, to Mr. Chow and then Dr. Montgomery and then to the Minister.

It's, I think, should be better known in the United States that Russia's budget, it's national budget, is 52 percent made up of energy revenues. I'm going to ask our staff to get information about the U.S. budget which is, I'm sure, considerably less. It's been written over the course of several years that Russia has continued to use what has been termed, it's not my term, but someone else termed this, energy blackmail, to ensure they keep their State coffers full.

Foreign policy reported over the last 20 years Russia has used this energy blackmail more than 40 times including countries such as Lithuania, who testified.

You know, Mr. Chow, you said that there's no silver lining, our, you know, our actions today might not take immediate effect.

Dr. Montgomery, you were a lot more bullish on your position.

So I'd like to ask you all what are the steps that, in your opinion, the U.S. should take to reduce Russia's influence, to reduce their quick access to cash, to promote policies that are not in our interest and not in the interest of Europe and democracies around the world?

Starting with you, Dr. Montgomery.

What are the 1 or 2 things that we should do?

Mr. MONTGOMERY. Thank you, Madame Chair.

I will stick to energy things that we could do.

The CHAIR. Yes.

Mr. MONTGOMERY. Because I don't——

The CHAIR. Right, energy.

Mr. MONTGOMERY. Offer myself as an expert on others and I'm sure there are many others that could accomplish what you're talking about as well.

I make it that based on your numbers revenues from natural gas are probably somewhere around 20 percent of energy revenues, 10 percent therefore of the Russian budget. If we could take out half of that well, that would be about 5 percent of their budget. I know what the budget committees and Congress would feel about that if it happened to the United States.

So I think that would be effective.

I agree with Mr. Goldwyn that it's the potential competition that is really important. It is. We see this in industry after industry where a monopolist restrains themselves because they know that if they go much above competitive pricing there are others who are not in the market now, but are ready to leap in. That's the position the United States needs to be in.

I agree with the Minister that the critical part for that is some form or another of removing the—of moving past the DOE process of making it clear that there is a policy commitment not to cap natural gas exports, not to stop that, not to prevent, you know, trades being made that are the advantage of both of our allies and ourselves. But also dealing effectively with potential problems with natural gas production, dealing with issues of shale gas and potential regulations that could hurt its production.

The CHAIR. OK.

Mr. Goldwyn, would you like to add anything?

Mr. GOLDWYN. Yes, please.

The CHAIR. Or disagree with anything that was said?

Mr. GOLDWYN. I don't disagree with what's said. I think there— I have a short list of 5 things I think the U.S. could do that could really reduce Russia's influence.

The first is diplomatic. We have a big agenda with Europe. If they integrate their gas market then they'll be able to move gas around and we'll be able to help more.

The second is I started a program called the Global Shale Gas Initiative when I was at the State Department. It's now called the Unconventional Gas Technology Program. We could do a lot more to provide technical assistance to other countries to help them develop their shale gas resources safely and efficiently.

I think the third thing, as we've talked about, obviously, would be to accelerate our ability to connect to the global market on gas.

I think we could encourage the Europeans to provide credit support to a lot of these projects in Europe. A lot of these economies are in bad shape as Dr. Montgomery and Dr. Chow know very well. They have a lot of work to do before people want to—before they can get prices right so people want to invest there. But I think the European Union could give credit support to a lot of those countries to enable them to build these interconnectors and projects.

I think we should, as we have for decades, encourage oil production both here at home and overseas because the more supply there is coming from Mexico or other places or even our own exports, if we get to a point where we can do that. We drive the global price of oil down. When the price of oil goes down, Russia's revenues are reduced and other countries have other choices of supply.

The CHAIR. Dr. Chow.

Mr. CHOW. Thank you, Madame Chair.

I actually don't disagree too much with what my colleagues have to say except in terms of timing and to be a little bit modest as to how much immediate impact that we can make while not perhaps attending to more urgent matters such as shoring up Ukraine.

In addition to what my colleagues have already said, I would emphasize the fact that our European allies are the ones with leverage over Russia on oil and gas imports, not us. Eighty percent of Russia's oil and gas exports go to Europe. They don't have many alternatives in the short to medium term. The pipelines to China are not built yet. Although Mr. Putin may be trying to do that when he visits China in May.

A number of the allies we met with, President Obama met with yesterday and today, have shale gas bans. We should send David back to Paris where there is an effective ban on even looking at exploring the resource that might be in France.

Germany has an effective ban on fracking. Germany, forty percent of Germany's gas demand comes from Russia.

So getting together with our allies to talk about what they can be doing in Europe to improve their own situation, as well as lessen their dependency on Russia, would be a very good thing in my mind.

The CHAIR. Thank you.

Senator Murkowski.

Senator MURKOWSKI. You'll get used to it.

[Laughter.]

The CHAIR. I like both of you so much.

Senator MURKOWSKI. Thank you.

The CHAIR. I work with both of you so closely.

Senator MURKOWSKI. I thank you madame chairman. It's good to have you as chair here next to my friend and our former chair, Senator Wyden.

To those on the panel, good morning and welcome. I apologize that I was tardy this morning, not because I wasn't anxious to hear the wisdom and the opinions of each of you. I thank you for your leadership in so many different areas.

I think it was you, Mr. Goldwyn, that mentioned that it's not whether in terms of exports, but whether we act in time to help. As I know some of you are aware I have really, a series of white papers after my energy 20/20 report from last year. We just released one about this narrowing window when it comes to our opportunities for export.

So when we talk about these issues I do think it is important to keep it in the context of timing.

I also recognize that we are in an enviable position as a Nation. The fact that we are having a hearing of this nature, talking about our energy opportunities for export from a position of abundance rather than one of scarcity which we so often seem to focus on. To be able to discuss our natural gas, our oil, our other resources as truly a strategic asset is something that, I think, is a remarkable story coming out of the United States. Our ingenuity that's driven by technologies is allowing us to access amazing resources in this country.

So it is a fabulous conversation to be having today.

I want to drill down a little bit here on the discussion of what we can do today to make a difference over in the Ukraine, have influence on Russia. The proposal or the discussion that we've been having about well, if in fact we were to accelerate the permitting process through DOE. In fact, that doesn't get gas to Ukraine or anywhere, at least for a couple years.

So therefore, if we can't do something by gosh, today to get our gas over across the water, then it's not worth doing.

I have suggested that it is about the signal that is sent, about the United States' role, our leadership role from a geopolitical perspective that is as instrumental as anything.

Mr. Chow, I think you used the term that it's irrelevant in the short run.

What I'd like to hear from each of you is how important is that signal that is sent if we are to accelerate our permitting through the DOE process?

Mr. Sieminski, if you can, kind of, speak to it from the pricing perspective? What does it mean, not only in Europe, but in Asia if we are to act more aggressively with the signals that come out of this Administration saying we're serious about being a player on the world scene? If we can truly just go down through the panel and each give your observations as to how significant a signal is as opposed to actual gas into our friends' and our allies' systems.

Mr. Sieminski, we'll start with you.

Mr. SIEMINSKI. Senator Murkowski, I think signals could certainly be important. They have to be followed up by concrete action to have, ultimately have, the impact, not be temporary.

Senator MURKOWSKI. By concrete action does it need to be more than an expedited process?

Mr. SIEMINSKI. For example the gas actually entering into the marketplace in some way. I think you could argue that the increase, the very strong increase in domestic production in the U.S. has already had some impact because our imports of natural gas are much lower now than they were projected to be just 5 years ago. So that's freed up other gas in the global markets to be available to other consumers like Europe and Asia.

The possibility that the U.S. would enter into the global markets with LNG exports after the completion of the LNG facility at Sabine Pass, I think has already had some impact on the psychology of long term contracts. There have been companies who have indicated that they have felt that they had more successful opportunities to negotiate with large gas suppliers for better contract terms than they would have had had the facility in Louisiana not already be under construction.

Senator MURKOWSKI. Let's quickly go down.

Minister Neverovič, how has—how would signals be received over in Lithuania and other Nations?

Mr. NEVEROVIČ. Yes, thank you very much for this question.

It's absolutely important signal which you can send. I can bring your attention to the fact that there are companies which trade in gas which already are moving to basically a pricing on more sport market model. But majority of the contracts are still being done on the basis of long term contracting, long term pricing.

So this is where it is important that any signal which is there, which is sent to the market, it could strengthen the buyers. They could feel more comfortable knowing that there will be more gas in the market. Then their position would be much stronger vis-&-vis the especially monopolist suppliers. That we don't have to attach ourselves to these long term contracts knowing that there will be gas on the market and possibly it will be more competitive.

So this signal would be very important I would say.

The CHAIR. If the 3 of you all would answer really quickly for the Senator. Just take 30 seconds each. Is it important? How important is a signal? Really quickly.

Mr. MONTGOMERY. Yes, I believe it's important. It's my opinion that we see evidence across economic markets that signals work. It's also important that they be credible. I think that's a great advantage of this kind of a signal because it's actually in our narrow economic interest to do, to facilate exports as well as strategic.

The CHAIR. Mr. Goldwyn.

Mr. GOLDWYN. I think from a diplomatic point of view, a signal is important for diplomatic, strategic reassurance. We spent decades trying to get other countries to provide gas to Europe. If we actually do it ourselves I think that would be powerful.

It impacts financing if you're accessing Henry Hub prices opposed to high priced Qatari. It's cheaper to provide, to get financing for those projects overseas.

Third, I think it would impact the market cap for Russian companies right now because if they have a lower market share or they're getting lower revenues than their prices on global markets will be lower.

I think it impacts price formation. Even Asian buyers, as Dr. Sieminski has indicated, are waiting to see if U.S. LNG will come into the market so they can get lower prices rather than oil linked prices.

So it's, you know, buy the rumor, sell the fact, whatever you're aphorism is, when we do things in the market today, those signals have immediate impact even if the end game is long term.

The CHAIR. Dr. Chow, really quickly and then I'm going to turn to Senator Wyden.

Mr. CHOW. I think the most important signal we can give right now in response to Russia's aggression in Ukraine is to strengthen Ukrainian economy. The Ukraine could be self sufficient in gas in a faster period of time than you can build a LNG terminal in Ukraine.

Ukraine, until the 1970s exported gas to the Russian republic. It is the corrupt, pervasive corruption, and inefficiency in the Ukrainian energy system that makes Ukraine vulnerable. Ukraine continues to transit more than 50 percent of Russia's gas to Europe.

If we strengthen Ukraine, that would be the most important signal to the Kremlin, it would seem to me.

Frankly, Senators, a billion dollar loan guarantee is a pretty feeble response to what has already happened.

The CHAIR. Senator Wyden.

Senator WYDEN. Thank you, Madame Chair.

Madame Chair I want to congratulate you. I think you're going to do a first rate job chairing the committee. I think the Landrieu/ Murkowski team, colleagues, all of us are going to be well served by having the 2 of them lead us.

Colleagues, in my view, yesterday's decision to approve the Jordon Cove facility in my home State reinforces my view that there is a sensible place between no energy exports and approving every application on offer. Now a year ago in this room that was called finding a sweet spot, where you factored in the needs of our manufacturers and our consumers and environmental questions and national security. My view is there still is a sweet spot recognizing that the geo-political and national security considerations have certainly changed in the last year.

36

Now yesterday's decision with respect to Jordan Cove shows the kind of considerations that need to go into this mix. For example, Jordan Cove is the only West Coast facility that is now on track for approval for exports. Also there will be less impact on American gas supply which is going to be important to our consumers. Senator Stabenow and others made this point because a portion of the gas for Jordan Cove will come from Canada, not going to be American supply.

So let me enlighten that. Kind of pick up on what Senator Murkowski was talking about with respect to the situation in Eastern Europe. In looking at the range of events surrounding Ukraine, I was struck by how the mention of potentially significant shale formations is coming up more often with respect to Eastern European countries. Poland and I'm sure there's going to be discussion of it in Lithuania.

Now everything I have learned and you touched on this, Mr. Chow, is that it's going to take a look of money and it's going to take a lot of time to build a LNG terminal. We're talking about years. We're not talking about months. We're talking about years to build one.

So my question and perhaps for you, Mr. Goldwyn and you, Mr. Chow. Wouldn't it be faster to export more of our knowledge more quickly to these countries in terms of how we can help get them, help them shake free of Russian oil and gas? Wouldn't that be the fastest way to move in a manner that really would help them shake free of Russian oil and gas? I think I really heard you touch on this, Mr. Chow.

Maybe you could amplify it and maybe we'll start with you, Mr. Chow and Mr. Goldwyn because exporting our knowledge could really make a difference quickly. I compare that to the years that it would take for a terminal and the expense.

Mr. Chow, first.

Mr. CHOW. Thank you, Senator.

It's not just shale gas. Actually you can increase conventional gas production faster in Ukraine. You don't have to wait for shale gas.

It's not only knowledge, but also of course, investment as well as managerial expertise. But before you can do that Ukraine needs to clean up its act in terms of its energy sector.

Today Ukraine imports gas from Russia around $300 per thousand cubic meters. It may go up to 400 by April 1st. It provides $40 per thousand cubic meter for the same gas but to domestic production.

So this incentivizes domestic production. All that needs to change. The reason is there. It's not an accident, as they say in that part of the world because it facilitates corruption.

For 20 years the Ukrainian energy sector have been hampered by corruption from the very, very top. So if we do anything at all we should condition our aid that we're considering giving Ukraine for both the IMF and other Western donors on fundamental structure reform of the energy sector.

Senator WYDEN. I heard you touch on this too, Mr. Goldwyn, in terms of what we could do in addition to what we're doing now to help these countries shake free of Russian oil and gas.

Your comments?

Mr. GOLDWYN. Great. Thank you, Senator Wyden. Thank you for your leadership on this issue.

I think we need to do both. There's no question that providing technical assistance to countries like Ukraine but also Romania, Bulgaria, Poland, Lithuania which has shales also, will help them develop those over time.

But Europe actually has a number of existing LNG importing terminals that have not used their maximum capacity. In fact Spain is kind of an island to the rest of Europe.

So that's why I think the process of interconnection in creating a unified gas market will enable countries like Ukraine to get gas from LNG imports before they need to build new terminals. You can do a lot with interconnection and more pipelines, reverse flows into places like Ukraine. So I think they need to do both.

I think the time scale for getting more LNG into Central and Eastern Europe can happen much more quickly than the time it takes to build a new import facility and the floating facility——

Senator WYDEN. My time is up. But I'm very interested in this speed question because it is fine to talk about this in the abstract. If you could get that to the Chair and the ranking minority member so it could be shared with all of us. For me the question is speed.

Thank you, Madame Chair.

The CHAIR. Thank you.

Senator Barrasso, I think or Senator Flake.

Senator Scott, yes, but Senator Barrasso?

Senator BARRASSO. OK. Thank you, Madame Chairman and congratulations to you and your new role leading this committee.

I appreciate your willingness to hold this hearing today. We have an excellent panel of witnesses and happy to hear from each of you and very much value your opinions.

I must point out that today's hearing on this is the third committee we've had hearing on liquefied natural gas exports in the last 2 and a half years. So we've had 3 of those, yet since our first hearing on LNG exports in November 2011 the Administration has continued to move, I believe, at a snail's pace. The Administration has used its discretion to approve only 7 applications to export LNG.

Meanwhile the Administration continues to sit on 24 pending applications. 13 of these applications have been pending for more than a year. I believe that the delays have been inexcusable.

So I think that we need hearings like this, but more importantly we actually need to vote. I think the Senate needs to take action on LNG exports.

Yesterday I filed an amendment to the Ukraine bill which would expedite LNG exports to Ukraine and to members of the North Atlantic Treaty Organization. These Nations are pleading for American natural gas. They want the Senate to actually act, to do something.

What we have heard from the Majority Leader is one excuse after another for why the Senate shouldn't act. Two weeks ago the Chairman of the Foreign Relations Committee arbitrarily blocked my amendment to the Ukraine bill. Other members of the majority have said the Administration should stop approving LNG exports altogether.

If my colleagues on this committee are serious about promoting LNG exports than we should call on the Majority Leader to actually let the Senate do its job. We should call on the Majority Leader to allow the Senate to vote on expediting LNG exports. This is one way that we can make progress on this issue.

Two days from now, on Thursday, this committee is going to be asked to vote on the nomination of Rhea Suh, to be Assistant Secretary of the Interior. She has called natural gas production, "easily the single greatest threat to the ecological integrity of the West." I believe if she is confirmed she could block access and would block access to our Nation's vast natural gas resources.

It's very difficult for me to understand why this committee would hold a hearing in support of LNG exports today yet be asked to vote to approve a natural gas opponent on Thursday. So I would urge you, Madame Chairman and our colleagues on this committee, to reject this nominee. The committee needs to send a strong message that we are all in support of natural gas not one in opposition to it.

Mr. Neverovič, in your testimony you explained that Lithuania is totally dependent on Russian natural gas. Lithuania, along with 3 other NATO allies and 3 other European Nations, is 100 percent dependent on Russian gas. You explained that you were here today, you say, to plead with Congress to do everything within our power to expedite release of our abundant natural gas resources into the world market.

You say that you hope the Administration will expedite LNG exports.

However, you also state that if the Administration fails to act then Congress should work to expedite the LNG exports.

Has the Administration given you, given Lithuania, any indication that it's actually going to expedite LNG exports?

Mr. NEVEROVIČ.. Thank you very much for this question. I had very good meetings also planned in a very short time, but still good meetings in Department of Energy and Department of State. We had a very good discussion where my interlocutors introduced their position on whether realizing LNG export.

As I understand their main preoccupation needs to find this sweet spot which Senator previously has mentioned and understanding the current situation, geo-politically in Eastern Europe. They are looking into ways to expedite this process of approving licenses.

However, I argued that it should made faster. These signals are important for countries like us which specifically are developing infrastructure which would allow us to bring gas from alternative supply. Then American gas which would appear on the world market would make a difference.

So I would continue to encourage both the Administration and Congress to do anything possible to speed up these processes here.

Senator BARRASSO. So they talked nice to you, but in fact they failed to give you the assurance that you hoped for that we would actually get the action. I would think that if the Administration isn't ready to make that commitment today that it is then dependent upon the Congress to act.

Mr. Goldwyn, in your testimony you stated that a clear signal from the U.S. that LNG exports will be available to European allies would put immediate pressure on Russia's market share. You explained some respected analysts have been too quick to dismiss the connection between U.S. LNG exports and increased European energy security. You've talked to that and answered questions related to that.

You go on to say that in dismissing that connection they make a number of mistakes. Would you please explain these mistakes to members of the committee?

Mr. GOLDWYN. I think some analysts say it won't matter to have U.S. LNG exports because they'll go to Asia and not Europe. I think that's a premature assumption to make.

For one, we don't know if Russia were to restrict gas exports to Europe might, no doubt, European gas prices would go up. European buyers, like other buyers, often put a premium on diversity of supply or security. So I think it's premature to make that judgment.

The second, I think, they downplay the impact on price formation because LNG buyers buy long term. Right now they're not buying for next year, they're buying for the 2016 or 2018 to 2022 period. So they're negotiating now for projects that will come online then and for long term projects.

So they're negotiating today for delivery in the future, like anything else that has a futures price. So when you increase future supply you provide certainty that U.S. supply will reach the market in a certain time. They're going to calculate that into global supply and adjust prices.

I think the third thing they underestimate is this impact on financing because, you know, like for all the projects the U.S. has approved only one has reached final investment decision. So who knows which of these are actually going to get financed? But if you're going to try and finance a project and you've got oil at Qatari prices or you're going to finance a project with Henry Hub, the cost of your project is lower if the cost of your gas is cheaper and the amount of money that you need is cheaper. So I think it impacts the finance ability.

Last, I think, it—the markets score prices for equity investment today based on future performance. If there is a clear signal that Russia's future market share will be less than as anticipated, then the price of Rosneft and, you know, after the price of Lukoil, the price of any of these companies which have publicly traded shares which are calculated in future income from gas or from oil into their projections will be impacted. Those scores happen today as long as we create certainty about tomorrow.

Senator BARRASSO. Thank you, Madame Chairman.

The CHAIR. Thank you very much.

Senator Udall.

Again, thank you for the bill that you've introduced along with Senator Begich.

Senator UDALL. Thank you, Madame Chair.

I want to start out by acknowledging and welcoming our new Chair, Senator Landrieu. She has a vast amount of energy expertise and a vast amount of energy.

[Laughter.]

Senator UDALL. She'll bring both of those to the committee.

I wanted to also acknowledge Minister Neverovič . and forgive me if I didn't get your name pronounced properly. But I did want to acknowledge that your country is small geographically, but it's an enormous country when it comes to your courage and resolve. America is proud to be your ally and we're well aware of the history of the Baltic States and all its various iterations.

So thank you for being here today.

I, too, want to acknowledge that I'm really pleased that Chairman Landrieu has focused her first hearing on such an important issue. Our Nation's clean burning and job creating natural gas should and can play an important role in strengthening global security. The ongoing crisis in Ukraine which we're discussing here today and of course, around the world, and Russia's threat to use its natural gas exports as a weapon shows why we need to responsibly develop our own natural gas reserves and expand our capacity to export this resource abroad.

I do share the frustration of many of my colleagues like Senator Barrasso that the Department of Energy has moved slowly. I can put it another way, has not moved more quickly to approve exports to non-FTA countries. That's why I introduced a bill just a few weeks ago that would end the current log jam at the Department of Energy by deeming export to all WTO countries to be in the public interest, in effect, approving the pending application queue.

This bill is bipartisan and bicameral. In fact shortly after introducing my legislation, my home State colleague, Representative Gardner, presented a virtually identical measure in the House which will be marked up soon. I welcome him in joining me in this effort.

I've made this point publicly and with the Secretary numerous times over the last few weeks. The crisis in Ukraine has refocused on how U.S. natural gas exports can stabilize global security. That's why I also will file my bill that will allow immediate DOE approval for the WTO countries as an amendment to the pending Ukraine Sanctions bill.

I do think the Department of Energy is finally heeding the calls that I put forth and others have put forth to approve additional LNG permits. As Senator Wyden mentioned yesterday, the Department approved a permit for the Jordan Cove facility, something that I've been pushing for. A real signal that we've made a difference in demanding action.

I'd like to thank the Department and Secretary Moniz for putting additional emphasis on global energy security and the importance of our allies as a part of their rationale for approval.

So in sum, I'm hopeful that this refocused emphasis on the energy security of energy exports will lead to even more movement from the Department of Energy in the coming weeks and months. After all there are still 24 permits pending.

With that let me turn to the witnesses. I want to direct this question to the panel.

Much of the focus of LNG exports has been at the DOE's review of applications. But isn't it true that even with DOE approval the volume of natural gas to be exported is dependent on many other economic and financial considerations as well as FERC approval for environmental and other considerations?

Would it be fair to say that the DOE approval simply gives the green light for a market driven process?

I would welcome comment from any of you on the panel.

Mr. Chow, you've, I think, shed some important light on some of the broader dynamics at play and maybe we'll start with you.

Mr. CHOW. Senator, thank you for your question.

As I said in my testimony there are lots of good reasons why we should proceed with serious consideration and maybe speeding up the process for licensing of crude exports as well as more LNG facilities.

I think one point that I would make is that in not only does it send a signal to the market, but the fact of the matter is that sweet spot that Senator Wyden mentioned, grows as the resource base estimates grow, as our ability to recover more from gas from the shale grows. So I imagine that it also sends a message to the market that the Department of Energy's confidence that we have sufficient resource to both entertain exports as well as meet domestic demand.

Senator UDALL. Mr. Goldwyn.

Mr. GOLDWYN. I would say the answer to your question is yes really. The DOE license is really just a license to market. It just says that you're able to go to customers who we don't have free trade agreements with and say that you can sell gas to them.

It's not an indication that you've made environmental clearance. That comes from FERC.

It's not an indication that you have got community assent to build a project where you want.

It doesn't mean you've got financing.

I think that's probably the challenge of the process right now is people score these DOE approvals like they're real projects, but they're not. All you need for the DOE approval is a letter and a stamp. You know, to get FERC approval you've got to have, you know, millions of dollars of environmental assessment and you have to have credible financing.

If I could, actually, I've written an alternative proposal at Brookings if I could enter for the record, called, "A Modest Proposal for Improving the Department of Energy Non-FTA LNG Export Application Process."

Mr. GOLDWYN. But essentially if you just let projects which had cleared FERC. They had a formal FERC application go to the head of the line then you would be accelerating projects which are not just licenses to market, but projects which have—are ready and are commercially mature.

I think that would solve a lot of this confusion about whether or not we're going to have 18 BCF a day in projects. We're not going to by just getting the DOE to give its approval to projects that are ready to go.

Senator UDALL. Mr. Sieminski, let me turn to you for a follow on question, the seasonality of natural gas prices.

LNG exports might be able to stabilize these fluctuations for consumers and producers. Of course in my home State of Colorado and across the Nation you see a surge in the winter. Would exports create an opportunity to maintain production levels during seasons of high demand?

Mr. SIEMINSKI. It's certainly possible. The availability of the storage that's associated with LNG export facilities might, some of that gas, might be available domestically. If prices got higher in the domestic markets than what the gas could get in the global markets that could have been a useful thing for example if there had been some way to get LNG quickly into Boston during the polar vortex.

Senator, back to your earlier question.

EIA believes that there are lots of factors that enter into the LNG export calculation including what oil prices are in the global markets, how quickly oil and gas prices converge, what the pace of growth in supply and demand is outside. So yes, I would also agree that there are many factors, both in the energy markets and in the financial markets that would come into play in determining whether an LNG export facility actually got built and used.

Senator UDALL. Thank you for that.

Madame Chair, thank you. Let's find this sweet spot that seems to be the phase.

The CHAIR. Thank you very much for bringing up the queue process.

Senator Murkowski and I are really focus on that because there are a lot of questions. Thank you, Mr. Goldwyn, your report will be submitted for the record, the one that you referenced in response to that question.

Alright, I think we have Senator Flake. I hope I'm not going out of order here.

I'm sorry, Senator Manchin is next. I'm going in order. I'm sorry, go ahead Senator Flake and then Senator Manchin.

Thank you.

Senator FLAKE. If he's changed sides that's alright.

[Laughter.]

Senator FLAKE. I mean, I'll take it.

The CHAIR. We will never allow that.

[Laughter.]

The CHAIR. Although he has tried on occasion. We will never allow it.

Senator FLAKE. Just checking.

Mr. Sieminski, give me a sense of the world market here for LNG. I visited, several years ago, a facility in Trinidad and Tobago. At that time most of that LNG was coming to the States. Now we're almost no longer a net importer, just barely a net importer.

Where is that going? What kind of margin do they operate under? Is some of that going back to South America or is it elsewhere in the Caribbean or is some of that going to Europe? What is the price point needed where existing natural gas facilities like this can export to Europe?

Mr. SIEMINSKI. I don't have those numbers right in front of me, but my guess is that gas from Trinidad and Tobago is going to European markets. There is also—there are a couple of terminals, LNG terminals, one in Chile, one in Mexico, that might be available. The LNG markets are developing very rapidly, but even with the estimates that EIA has made for U.S. LNG exports, it's still a fairly small portion of the global LNG market. There are many other competitors in that market including Australia, Indonesia, some of the West African countries and others who are entering the markets.

Senator FLAKE. I'm just wondering, somebody, maybe Dr. Goldwyn, if you could tell me how will Russia react if we were to start permitting process, the signal was sent, prices drop. Will Russia act much like OPEC did earlier or does or any cartel in this fashion that they will lower prices to discourage investment in other facilities elsewhere?

How will Russia react here? At what point, how much lower will their prices have to be in order to discourage investment that needs to happen in these other countries including the U.S."

Mr. GOLDWYN. Thank you for the question, Senator.

I only went to law school, I didn't get my PhD. My wife did, so I can't claim the doctor.

But I think, well first, Russia has not shown any ability because it doesn't control enough of world supply to try and lower its prices to impact other's investments. But Russia has had to lower its prices in order to save its market. So as Dr. Sieminski and Dr. Montgomery both explained, the surplus of LNG when we stopped importing it forced Russia to renegotiate a lot of its long term contracts with Europe because they were able to buy spot.

So that was one impact.

They also had this famous Shtokman project where they thought they were going to be a major LNG export. The fact that they didn't have our market anymore made their project too expensive. So it wasn't so much they're deciding that they were going to kill investment elsewhere by lowering prices and getting more market share. It's that they were going to lose market share to the spot market, you know, if they didn't lower their prices.

So we're about to see, with Russia's negotiation with China, whether in fact they will lower their prices or lower their correlation between gas and oil prices in order to save market share. They've been negotiating for China for a huge pipeline, 40 BCM. Frankly in terms of China's dependence, something we need to worry about a little bit.

But they've been at loggerheads for years over price. This June, we're going to see if the Russians are going to cave. My guess is that they will. They will lower their correlation. They will agree to a better price deal, not because they're trying to kill our investment, but because they have no other choice.

That's the trend that we want to drive further because that just squeezes their cash-flow.

Senator FLAKE. Right. That's important. I just wondered how big their market share is or how—what ability they have to actually lower prices and undercut investment elsewhere but not as much.

Dr. Montgomery or somebody else, Ukraine, itself, because of corruption and Mr. Chow you mentioned their inability to produce their own whether it's shale gas or traditional gas. If they were to ramp up production significantly can they become—how quickly could they become completely independent of Russian gas or could they?

Yes.

Mr. CHOW. I don't think it's the aim necessarily is to be completely independent of Russian gas, but not to be so dependent on Russian gas. They're currently 60 percent dependent on Russian gas in an economy that's very gas heavy. Fourty percent of primary energy in Ukraine comes from natural gas. So that dependency on Russia is very significant.

I think to get about a 50 percent self sufficiency level Ukraine can probably do it within 2, 3 years with the right kind of policies and the right kind of investments.

Senator FLAKE. That's likely a combination of production increases and conservation measures that are highly inefficient, I understand, in terms of the use of gas.

Mr. CHOW. Certainly efficiency would help.

Right now their demand has come down mainly because of the collapse of the domestic economy not because of efficiency improvement. So when the economy grows some of that demand will come back, although creating greater GDP with the use of the same amount of gas.

Senator FLAKE. Thank you.

Thank you, Mr. Chair.

The CHAIR. Thank you very much.

Senator Manchin.

Senator MANCHIN. Thank you, madame chairman and thank all of you for your presentations today.

I want to thank first of all, Senator Landrieu and congratulate her on her first hearing as our new chairman of this committee. Look forward to working with her on truly creating an all of the above national energy policy.

Also I brought, at the time Chairman Wyden and Ranking Member Murkowski, to the State of West Virginia to see an all of the above energy policy that we use in our State. We try to use everything we have, our coal, our gas, our wind, our solar, everything. We think it's most needed as far as a policy for this country also.

My home State of West Virginia has been blessed, as you know, to have a little bit of everything. We use everything that we have also. I believe that we need to do that more in this country and look at a way to be more energy independent by using all and not writing one off against the other.

So what I would do, as I would like to ask a question to Mr. Sieminski.

Sir, with the Polar Vortex that we just had and basically the EIA saying that we're going to be needed fossil coal for the next 2, 3, 4 decades. You know the problems that we're having with EPA as far as producing that coal here in America. Are you concerned about the mix that we're having right now, the utilities are having, the mix of their portfolio and the—I'm told that we were very critically close to having some real serious black outs or brown outs during this Polar Vortex because of the coal fired plants that are going offline.

Mr. SIEMINSKI. There were some electricity issues in New England, mainly because of the growing dependence of New England on natural gas to fire their plants and the pipeline constraints getting gas into New England. Some of that was dealt with by the switching to fuel oil.

In EIA's longer term projections we actually have coal consumption just coming off a little bit. That is on the basis of existing law and regulation which does include things like the mercury air toxic rule and so on.

One of the interesting things, Senator, that you brought up and I might just add since we're talking and the question was asked, is there something that Europe could do? As you know the U.S. has been exporting coal to Europe.

Senator MANCHIN. If it wasn't for the export market we'd have no market in West Virginia.

Mr. SIEMINSKI. Right.

In fact the all of the above strategy that you indicated that the Administration is pursuing here in America is one that probably makes sense for many countries.

Senator MANCHIN. Do you truly believe that we are pursuing an all of the above energy policy?

Mr. SIEMINSKI. I'm going to stay out of the policy.

Senator MANCHIN. OK, I figured you would.

[Laughter.]

Mr. SIEMINSKI. But EIA, back to your question of the energy mix.

Senator MANCHIN. You've been pretty straight forward on EIA. What is it going to take to run this country?

Mr. SIEMINSKI. EIA's—what we see is natural gas and renewables growing faster than some of the others.

Senator MANCHIN. But natural gas and coal, even for the next 2 to 3 decades, is going to be——

Mr. SIEMINSKI. Right.

Senator MANCHIN. Seventy, 75 percent of the energy production that we need. Anyone that doesn't think that's true they are deniers.

Mr. SIEMINSKI. Right.

But the overall mix of fuels in the U.S. changes somewhat, but we're still, even in 2040 going to be very reliant on fossil fuels for our energy consumption.

Senator MANCHIN. You've got to tell some of our friends that truly don't want to hear the facts of what we're dealing with in the country and how we can do it much better. There's more demand around the world than ever before, right, for fossil?

Mr. SIEMINSKI. Demand.

Senator MANCHIN. It's growing, yes?

Mr. SIEMINSKI. Demand in general is rising very rapidly. We think overall energy demand between now and 2040 is going to be up by more than half. A lot of that growth, half of that growth is going to be in 2 countries, China and India alone. So it's going to be a challenge, Senator, to fill that——

Senator MANCHIN. A little bit better policy for global climate if we basically were using the technology that we have been able to reduce to particulates in this country and make, through our trade policies being used in other countries that are polluting more.

Mr. SIEMINSKI. One of the things that I've been asked in the past is when you look back at EIA's forecast 3 or 4 years ago and back to 2011, you know, had we seen demand increases for natural gas and how does that relate back to the export question.

Yes, we do see higher demand, but our supply numbers look even more robust. What that suggests is that there is ample gas for both domestic and exports.

Senator MANCHIN. I could, Mr. Neverovič, if I may ask you, do you all believe that you have the, I mean, geological deposits to where we could explore more and do more, more development, in your country and other European countries that would give you more freedom as far as from Russia's grip?

Mr. NEVEROVIČ. Thank you very much for your question.

I certainly believe that we should investigate. Then if we have such gas deposits we should explore them.

I had learned that in U.S. for shale gas revolution to happen it took many support from Department of Energy to investigate how to get out this shale gas. It took 30 years for this revolution to happen. So it's hard to expect that in Europe or for this matter in Lithuania it could be possible to do this very quickly, even considering that we can have the possibility to use your know how.

We need to have this learning process both on the level of Administration and also on the level of local communities where unfortunately usually some groups which are presenting shale gas investigation or exploration as a threat, major threat, to local communities which is usually not the case. With appropriate protection for the environment it's possible to investigate.

So I think after we get through all this legal environment adjustment so that investment is encouraged it will be possible to do it in Lithuania. It's already happening in other European countries.

Senator MANCHIN. Thank you.

The CHAIR. Thank you. Thank you so much.

Senator Stabenow and then Senator Baldwin and we'll be wrapping up about 12 o'clock.

Senator STABENOW. Thanks very much and congratulations, again, on chairing the committee. Looking forward to working with you.

I do want to take a few moments because it's a perspective not represented here today on the committee to talk about not only the U.S. energy revolution, but the fact that we also need to make sure it's coupled with U.S. manufacturing revolution. We note, we've been talking a lot about signals today, sending signals overseas. It's also important to send a signal to American manufacturers who are looking at bringing jobs home because of low energy prices to make sure that there's a signal for them as well because the low energy prices, Madame Chair, that you've been talking about, really are making a difference in terms of creating jobs here at home in manufacturing.

I welcome each of you and to have our Minister of Energy, welcome to each of you.

But I think it is important to put, for the record that last month there was a study by the Charles River Associates. They found that using our own low cost natural gas to increase American manufacturing output is twice as valuable to our overall economy and creates 8 times as many jobs as sending this important American resource overseas.

I'm not suggesting that we should cap or end exports. What I am advocating for is a thoughtful, balanced approach, as others have said, to make sure we find the sweet spot. We've still got 10 million people out of work in this country. People know that manufacturing jobs are good jobs for us.

So I think we have an important balance to do.

With Monday's announcement the DOE has now approved 6 export facilities with a capacity of over 9 billion cubic feet per day. I think it's really important that we move forward with the right kind of analysis about the impact on prices. We don't know for sure. I'm concerned that as we've looked at updating studies that the company building an export facility actually funded the update of the NERA study. So I think there are other perspectives that are important.

We have a study from Purdue University that found that LNG exports between 6 and twelve billion cubic feet a day result in declining American GDP and higher energy prices for consumers. The Purdue study concludes that while the natural gas sector benefits from more exports. Other industries and residential consumers lose out due to high energy costs.

I think it's important. We can debate that. That may be true, that may not be true. It may be it's not true. It may be that as we move forward we will find that we can do both as the panel has talked about which would be the best of both worlds to be able to do that.

But I do believe that the DOE should conduct a new study on the economic impacts of exports and move forward in a thoughtful way because of the impact on the American economy. I'm deeply concerned about what's happening in Ukraine. I do not underestimate what is happening around the world. But I also know what is happening here at home, what is happening here at home with 10 million people out of work and a renaissance in manufacturing leading our recovery that is so very important.

The Boston consulting group concluded that affordable natural gas prices could lead to 5 million more manufacturing jobs by the end of the decade.

The American Chemistry Council has identified 120 newly announced chemical and plastics manufacturing projects with over 100 billion investment. This is great news for us.

Yet NERA's study did not include these projects nor does the EIA's 2013 Annual Energy Outlook which NERA used to update its study.

So I just think it's important to say that for the record. Will get in a question.

That is, all of you talk greatly about this being long term as we look at developing export potential. So first I think it is important to talk about it will take several years to get something online. Once they're approved it's up to private companies to decide where to send the gas. They'll decide based on market pressures.

So it seems to me when we look at the fact that in Asia right now prices are nearly $16 million per million BTUs verses Europe where prices are $10 per BTUs. I'm sorry, per million BTUs.

I would ask Mr. Chow wouldn't you think a company would want to go to the highest bidder? Chances are our natural gas will be going to Asia?

Mr. CHOW. While that may be true, Senator, I also think that we will continue to maintain a level of competitiveness in this country because we have the advantage of being sitting at the source of that gas rather than having to spend $4 to $6 per million BTUs just to liquefy and transport that gas and regassification. So some level of competiveness edge will be retained in the U.S.

The other point I would want to make to you is that to consider that long term investors in manufacturing also need to know that there will be a stable supply of gas that's available.

Senator STABENOW. Absolutely.

Mr. CHOW. We have had times in this country when the natural gas price dropped so low as to make us concerned about long term viability of sustaining that supply when it dropped below $3 per million BTU. Where that sweet spot is is for elected officials and policymakers to make, not for foreign analysts.

Senator STABENOW. Thank you.

Madame Chair, I know my time is up. I look forward to working with you, but I do think, you know, this is not easy. I don't support stopping exports or capping exports, but I do think it's important that we move forward in a thoughtful way.

The CHAIR. Thank you, Senator. I appreciate that. We will get to the bottom of these facts.

Senator Scott, who was here first, we will recognize you, then Senator Baldwin and Senator Hoeven and then Senator Murkowski and I will do some closing questions. It's been an excellent hearing so far.

Thank you, Senator Scott for being here so early. I know you had to slip out so we're happy for your questions now.

Senator SCOTT. Thank you, Madame Chairwoman. Thank you for holding this hearing today and thank you to the panelists for being a part of the conversation which is, obviously, a very timely conversation as we look at this as a geopolitical tool using our resources in an effective way.

I think it's also important to note that later this week the committee will hold an important vote for the future of American natural gas production with the nomination of Ms. Rhea Suh to become the Assistant Secretary for Fish, Wildlife and Parks. In fact it's almost hard to ignore the dichotomy that exists between the strong support for natural gas and production and the LNG exports that have been displayed at this hearing and Ms. Suh's stated opposition to increase natural gas production.

My first question to Dr. Montgomery or Mr. Goldwyn is that in both of your testimonies you've essentially said that an immediate announcement of unlimited LNG exports by the U.S. would signal competition to Russia that could impact their contract prices with Europe. Do you think the same could be said or is true if the U.S. immediately allowed crude oil exports as well?

Dr. Montgomery.

Mr. MONTGOMERY. Thank you, Senator Scott.

I think that both crude oil exports and natural gas exports can serve to diminish Russia's revenues and therefore would have an effect. I think that it's less a matter of immediacy in terms of crude oil verses natural gas than of magnitude. I think in both cases, yes, the importance of the announcement is that it establishes expectations over the longer term, as Mr. Goldwyn was saying about what terms natural gas would be available over the, you know, the long term contracts that people are now signing. Over that term we can look at pretty substantial LNG exports being possible and having substantial effect on Russia.

At this point our issue with crude oil exports appears to be more one of the mismatch between the light crudes that we are producing——

Senator SCOTT Shale.

Mr. MONTGOMERY. In our complex refineries.

I'm not sure whether—and so I think an announcement of crude oil exports that, you know, a policy toward crude oil exports would certainly have a signaling effect. We're just starting to work on the subject to try to understand how large a magnitude that might have. It has to go in the right direction.

If we allow crude oil exports it will mean more crude production in the United States. If there's more crude production in the United States that tips the balance, more supply, less demand, lower world oil prices, that has benefits in many ways in depriving strategic rivals and clearly declared enemies of revenues.

Senator SCOTT. Yes, it's a consistent formula that produces a consistent result it seems.

Mr. Goldwyn.

Mr. GOLDWYN. Yes, I agree with Dr. Montgomery. Directionally the more we export crude oil or condensate we will increase global supply and put pressure particularly on brand prices and that's what a lot Russian crudes are priced to. Right now at Brookings we have a task force on accessing crude oil exports. In fact we've commissioned NERA and Dr. Montgomery to do the econometric study, much as was done on LNG exports because everyone is asking this question about whether there will be a day of reckoning.

I think it's clear that there will be a day of reckoning when we will maximize how much we can use light, tight oil in our refineries or to Canada or topping. Then it will start to impact production negatively.

The question of when that day of reckoning is is a complicated answer that we need some serious analysis. We hope by June that we'll have that study from NERA and a Brookings Task Force report to address exactly that question.

Senator SCOTT. I only have about a minute left so I'll skip to my last question for Dr. Montgomery.

Would you call natural gas production the single greatest threat to the ecological integrity of the West and if the Obama Administration or any Administration held that view how could that mindset impact natural gas production in the future of U.S. LNG exports?

Mr. MONTGOMERY. I do not think it is that natural gas production is a major ecological threat. I think that natural gas production can be carried out in an environmentally sensitive way that avoids harm to ecologically important regions that's consistent with wildlife preservation.

My son lives in Colorado too. He's an avid environmentalist. He works doing oil and gas exploration.

I think there is a great deal of misinformation and sheer fear mongering about the effects of shale gas production, many of the claims being completely untrue. I've tried to study the geology here is just expert opinion is quite clear that fracking does not produce ground water problems. The problems, if they exist, are because of waste water disposal practices.

But anyway, without getting into the details, it is clear industry wants to solve this problem. They've worked closely with the Governor of Colorado to develop a set of regulations that they agree, in a bipartisan way. I'm sorry Senator Udall isn't here to take credit for this too.

It can be done without—I mean, everything we do has a risk. But it can be done with nothing more than manageable risks to the environment.

Senator SCOTT. Thank you, Dr. Montgomery.

Madame Chairwoman——

The CHAIR. Thank you very much.

Senator Baldwin, thank you for your extraordinary patience. You've been here early the whole morning. Just in order of seniority we find you toward the end. But thank you very much for being attentive.

Senator BALDWIN. Thank you.

Let me start out by congratulating you, Chair Landrieu, on your new role. It is great to see you in the Chair. I look forward to our work together in the years to come.

I want to associate myself with some of the comments made by Senator Stabenow before she had to depart because, you know, they say all politics is local. When you think about it this is obviously a large country and I think it's fair to say that, as with other energy issues, the polices that we're discussing today don't necessarily affect all of our States in an even manner.

Like Senator Stabenow's State, Wisconsin is one of the leading manufacturing States in the United States. In fact I think right now it can boast the role of No. 1 manufacturing State as a percent of our overall economy. I note because of the focus of today's hearing that we don't have a witness that's representing consumer voices today. Obviously they are a very important part of this weighty discussion. So I look forward to future opportunities to hear from those witnesses also.

Mr. Sieminski, I'd like to ask you a few questions this morning. Or—well, no, it is still this morning.

[Laughter.]

Senator BALDWIN. Just checking.

The paper industry is a major part of Wisconsin's manufacturing and economy. Our paper companies are working hard to compete in a very trade sensitive, trade impacted industry while also complying, obviously, with environmental quality standards that some of their, well most of their foreign competitors do not face. Paper mills that would like to switch over to natural gas have been unable to secure a supply of fuel because of inadequate infrastructure.

Many companies don't have adequate access to natural gas. Yet today we're, of course, talking about increasing our exports of natural gas.

So my first question for you is how will increased exports impact the construction of gas infrastructure for companies, that companies in Wisconsin might be able to rely on?

Mr. SIEMINSKI. Senator Baldwin, let me just start off by saying that in EIA's reference case forecast we have natural gas consumption in the paper industry overall nearly doubling between 2010 and 2040. In general we have very strong growth in industrial natural gas consumption. I don't think that there is a shortage of gas in a sense that would lead to problems in the manufacturing industries.

On the issue of infrastructure——

Senator BALDWIN. Yes.

Mr. SIEMINSKI. Which you asked about. You know, there is the Secretary of Energy's, Secretary Moniz, has a big and the President have a quadrennial energy review underway that intends to directly address these infrastructure issues.

Let me back up just a second and start with on the issue of natural gas production in the U.S. there is no dispute that I can find in the economic literature on either, you know, side of this that the positive impacts on jobs and GDP from the production activity are really strong.

On the jobs impact of exports the literature is somewhat mixed. But interestingly it seems to be relatively minor.

So the impacts on GDP and the impacts on jobs from exports are small because the exports are a small proportion of the overall production in the U.S. and the overall global markets.

The—one of the things that I think Mr. Chow said that I'd like to come back to is that U.S. manufacturers are always, you know, anybody that's an industrial consumer of gas or even electric utility consumer of gas is always going to have an advantage over a global LNG market which is going to tend to go into—it's going to be 2 or 3 times higher in price than the average price for gas at the well head in the U.S.

So then if we come back to the question of well, what is the difficulty that you're having in your State of Wisconsin with the paper industry being able to get gas. I think it's really not so much a question of the overall availability of gas. It's how do you get those pipelines built to take the gas from where it is to get it into those companies?

That's something that the utilities and the companies themselves are going to have to work out. I think that the intent of the quadrennial energy review is to try to see if there are any policy bottlenecks that could help in that area.

Senator BALDWIN. I would, if I might, Chair Landrieu, my time has run out and I did want to ask some other questions.

But on that comment, you have perhaps a deep skepticism this particular year. I'm going to switch fuels for a second. But having been told that there were adequate supplies of propane at a time when there were incredible increases in exports we had a dire emergency where a quarter million people were having trouble heating their homes in Wisconsin. A lot of it had to do with that

52

transfer, that infrastructure and being diverted for more profitable fuels so that they could, you know, even change directions and put other fuels in them.

So, you know, being able to respond to this need in manufacturing is going to be real critical to our domestic employment, our domestic economy.

Thank you. I note my time has run out.

The CHAIR. Thank you very much.

Senator, I've committed to you and Senator Franken who continually have raised this issue. It's very important to the people of Wisconsin, of course and Minnesota. We don't heat our homes the same way that you do. We normally don't have to. This winter has been an exception. But we will be doing some kind of hearing on that to help you all, to help us figure that out.

Senator Hoeven.

Senator HOEVEN. Thank you, Madame Chairman. Also, I want to congratulate you on your new position as chairman of this committee and express that I look forward to continuing to work with you.

To the good Senator from Wisconsin, we're flaring off huge amounts of natural gas in my State. We would love nothing better than to bring more of it to you and to others.

My question to our panelists starting with Mr. Sieminski is right now the European Union gets about a third of its natural gas from Russia. I would like each of you to tell me how you think we can help the EU reduce its dependence on Russian gas.

Mr. SIEMINSKI. Again Senator, EIA is a statistical agency and not a policy agency so I'm not going to offer policy prescriptions other than to say that the all of the above energy strategy seems to make sense for the United States. It might make sense for other countries.

One thing that I can say in terms of EIA's data is that the growth in supply that we're seeing over the last few years is extraordinary and it leaves an opportunity for both growth in domestic consumption of natural gas as well as exports.

Senator HOEVEN. Sir.

Mr. NEVEROVIČ. Thank you for the question.

The problem that we have is that we have a fragmented and closed markets in some of the EU countries. Lithuania is one of those countries. As I said, we are dependent 100 percent on supply from Gazprom.

So what we have to do at our home to address this problem is to diversify, to create alternative routes of supply. That is our LNG floating ship which will help to bring gas from alternative direction.

But then there is a question of where do we get the gas because, of course, diversification would serve already the purpose of having more objective price than to for monopoly not being able to charge this margin of a closed market. But on the other hand increased and newly created global gas market would definitely help to bring down those prices, globally.

So this would be definitely the direction which all actions on the part of the U.S. Government and Congress could help and specifically liberalizing LNG exports.

53

Senator HOEVEN. Thank you, Minister.

Dr. Montgomery.

Mr. MONTGOMERY. Yes, I think that U.S. exports of LNG, wherever they go in the world, will help to reduce Europe's dependence on Russia even if our exports go to Asia and are competing with exports that Russia might be sending through a pipeline to China. That frees up other gas to move to Europe so that, you know, it, you know, we look in the long run in the global market where if we put gas into it, it is going to be benefiting Europe eventually.

That Europe would then be facing either a chase into Russia who has to accept lower prices for gas or be less physically dependent on the Russian gas. I'm not quite sure which way it will play out.

Senator HOEVEN. Thank you, Doctor.

Mr. Goldwyn.

Mr. GOLDWYN. Six steps, Senator.

First we should encourage the European Union to complete the integration of a gas market so you can move gas from Spain all the way to Kiev.

Second we should encourage——

Senator HOEVEN. They have a fair amount of that in place already, don't they?

Mr. GOLDWYN. A fair amount. But actually it's very hard to move gas from point to point. Although they've eliminated the destination clauses there's enough pipeline capacity to move from the Iberian Peninsula into the rest of Europe. So they need more pipelines there.

You have to negotiate the entry and exit price at each point along the pipeline. So it's, you know, it can be up to 10 steps to figure out where it is. They're not transparent about capacity of those pipelines either. So there's more work that they could do which would really make it easier for LNG to get into that system from whatever terminal it comes into.

So the gas market is No. 1.

Interconnections, I would say, are No. 2.

Getting prices right internally which the hedge I always talked about at length is important both to control demand and also to attract investment.

Promoting indigenous gas, shale gas, in countries in Europe.

Enhancing energy efficiency and renewables in places where that's appropriate in Europe.

Accelerating the consideration of applications to export U.S. LNG.

The CHAIR. Mr. Chow, before you answer. Would you all put that graph up because this will explain some things that you all are talking about? This is the pipeline system in Europe. Both of you all are commenting on it.

Senator HOEVEN. I think that's an interesting point particularly with the Energy Minister's meeting now.

The CHAIR. Would you please, yes.

Senator HOEVEN. In is it April on this very issue?

The CHAIR. Could you all explain? Just, that's fine. Just hold it up there.

The blue are the already constructed gas pipelines, correct?

Staff? Yes.

The red are proposed oil, gas.

Mr. Goldwyn and Mr. Chow, look at this map and just comment 1 minute in answer of Senator Hoeven's question which I think is important. Is Europe integrated with its gas pipeline?

Go ahead, Dr. Chow.

Mr. CHOW. It is not and for 2 basic reasons.

One, the infrastructure is not necessarily connected as well as it needs to be.

Two is market practices. The fact that you have incumbents in some of these countries while also trying to protect their own monopoly power and not let gas and electricity flow freely across the continent is a big problem in Europe.

You're right, Senator. The U.S./EU Energy Council will be meeting next month, I believe in Europe.

Senator HOEVEN. Right. So this is certainly an area where they can do some substantive work.

Mr. CHOW. I would add one more, Madame Chair, if am I allowed, which is they really need to look at developing further their own energy resources in Europe beyond renewables which they do a good job in.

But why not look at the resources, particularly in oil and gas, but also coal that is in Western Europe already that they're not taking advantage of rather than importing those resources from faraway places. That's something they can do to help themselves very much.

I think I have a sense of irony that it is the Central and Eastern European countries who are most dependent on Russia for its oil and gas today who wants to take the strongest position on Russia because of the aggression that it has caused in Ukraine as opposed to the Western European countries who are, by definition, more diversified, who are reluctant to respond to Russia's aggression.

So something that we can do to get our allies and ourselves on the same page in that area is certainly something that's worth doing in the coming days and weeks.

Senator HOEVEN. Madame Chairman.

The CHAIR. A very important insight.

Senator HOEVEN. I apologize I know I'm over my time, but if I could beg your indulgence.

On that point, Mr. Chow and maybe Mr. Goldwyn wants to weigh in here as well. I visited with companies like Exxon, Chevron, Shell and others that are willing to do more both onshore but also offshore in the Black Sea as well as companies like Statoil that are doing a lot of oil and gas development, obviously, in the North Sea and so forth.

What about their ability in the near term here to provide more natural gas to these counties? Is there something we can do to help make that happen?

Mr. GOLDWYN. I would say with respect to the Norwegians, they do have search capacity to move more gas. At times over the last year and a half or so they have been the larger supplier of gas over Gazprom. So they have the ability. There's really nothing we need to do in order to help them capture that market.

But on the other 2 points something I would echo what Ed Chow has said. We could be a lot more forthright in, you know, and less timid about encouraging unconventional and conventional gas development in Europe.

I've been to 8 of those countries trying to teach safe shale gas practices to regulators over there. They don't have private ownership. They don't have access to infrastructure. In places like Bulgaria, you've got Gazprom actively undermining development there.

So technical assistance, getting regulators comfortable, those are things we are doing, but we could do a lot more of.

The second one I think is the point Ed made and that Chair Landrieu has made with the map is really important. The European story is that we eliminated destination clauses. We're done. We have an integrated gas market. It's just not the case.

There's much more work that needs to be done. I've talked to my colleagues at the State Department and encouraged them to put that at the top of their agenda because you get that market unblocked you get more connections between there. You don't strand Iberian gas. You get connections between Lithuania and Latvia.

You can move a lot more gas around that continent a lot faster than it takes to build a new LNG export terminal. You can use the ones that they've got.

The CHAIR. This has been an excellent hearing. We're going to have to bring it to a close.

I have just one or 2 comments and questions and turn it over to Senator Murkowski for final remarks.

But I want to thank you all for your patience, you excellent testimony. Of course, everything will be submitted to the record.

But let me just bring this back locally, to the U.S. and particularly to Louisiana and the energy coast. Designing an energy policy, which this committee will be focused on, promoting America as an energy super power will create thousands and thousands of jobs here at home and abroad and will help us promote democracy which is one of the central principles of the existence of our Nation.

I know that we've spent a lot of time talking about Europe and the Ukraine. But we've also started this hearing by talking about the 37,000 jobs in Louisiana and Texas and the Gulf Coast that can be created right now with the production and opening up of exports for liquefied natural gas.

Let me also assure my colleagues, mostly Senator Stabenow and Senator Baldwin, who were very respectful and appropriate in their comments. I want to be the same. Louisiana is the second largest producer of gas in this country, offshore and on. But we're also the third largest consumer of gas.

It is certainly not in this Senator's interest to promote a policy where the prices would skyrocket and put our consumers at a disadvantage. We have industrial consumers, commercial consumers, residential consumers.

But the facts are and I think the case has been made overwhelmingly by a variety of different reports that opening up export markets helps to increase domestic supply, not close it down, increase it, of gas and natural gas.

It also will help to create jobs here at home and abroad.

The price, as you all said, Louisiana, Louisiana—the U.S. because it's North Dakota production, Texas, Oklahoma, Colorado, will always have an advantage because we are the source of the product.

Now, yes, does thought have to go into it? Is it the silver bullet, you know, the silver bullet? No. But it's part of, I think, the equation of how to create jobs at home, promote America's strength abroad.

The 3 questions I have and we're not going to take time. I may just ask you all to submit these in writing for the committee.

One other thing that we can export and Alaska is proud of this. Louisiana and Texas are proud of this, is our technology. It's not just our gas and oil that we can export, both refined and crude, but our technology.

What could we do better as a country? We're going to do these answers in writing. To encourage technology, not just from the big oil companies that, of course, have their own ability to do that. But the thousands of small, independent producers that sometimes find it difficult to work overseas. How could we assist them to, you know, to promote and export their technology which is value added to American inventors, etcetera?

That's one question for the writing.

The other is we've talked a lot about America. I'd like to talk about North America. I'd like to talk about the power of Canada, America and Mexico as a major energy producer and supplier. What's recently happened is a game changer with the government of Mexico moving for the first time to privatize their energy sector.

So they're reducing their corruption, opening up the private market. Mexico is a really big place with a lot of big promise. It sits very close to us. I'd like our country to start thinking about Mexico.

Of course, building the keystone pipeline, in my view, and using Canada and Mexico, the North American alliance of energy is a powerful, powerful tool.

Finally I don't want to underestimate my colleague that's Senator Barrasso, you know, says that if we would just streamline these processes. Yes. I'm for streamlining. I'm for expediting.

But I also hope that critics of the Administration will focus on what can we do to help the Ukraine minimize its corruption. What can we do to, you know, enhance the $1 billion that you said, Mr. Chow, was just a drop in the bucket.

For the record you should submit what you think a significant investment to the Ukraine would be that would send the most positive signal.

So while there's a lot of criticism going around from one side to the Administration. I would also like to go on record saying for my colleagues and this is not Senator Murkowski, but others on the Republican side, put your money where your mouth is. You want to help, let's step up with some additional funding to help the Ukraine and not just blame somebody else because permits are going a little slowly.

I'll let you have the last word.

Senator MURKOWSKI. Thank you, Madame Chairman.

This has been, I think, a great hearing. Certainly a good way to kick off your first full committee hearing as chair on an issue that is clearly timely and I think holds so much promise for America's position in the world as an energy leader.

Again, an opportunity for us as a Nation to wield some influence in a positive way and a way, you started off the questioning talking about Russia and energy blackmail. I don't think that the U.S. would ever assert that they would come at it from that kind of a dictatorial type of a position, but one where we can help our friends and allies. One where we can engage in an environment where as we seek to increase production domestically how that influences and positively impacts those around the globe, all things being equal, you know, all are benefited by the U.S. and our increasing role, our increasing presence in this market.

I wanted to ask one very, very quick question. This relates to the issue that Senator Barrasso brought up with the amendment that he had attempted to advance in foreign relations. As you know, we have the Ukraine legislation on the Floor in front of us and the push from Senator Barrasso and others to extend the FTA fast tracking to NATO and WTO members.

There has been the issue raised of potential trade violations based on this expedited treatment to NATO members and other specific countries like Japan, but not to all WTO members.

Can anybody speak to that issue in terms of whether or not you believe that it does present a trade violation?

Mr. Goldwyn.

We all look to you, so you get to step up.

Mr. GOLDWYN. I'm the lawyer and not——

I confess to not having, being familiar with all the text to the bill. But I think to the extent that we have a trade agreement with a country and we adopt a practice which excludes anybody that we have that kind of a trade agreement with then we could be accused of discriminatory practice and violation of it.

Now I don't know when you looked at which version of the bill whether it covers everybody that we have a trade agreement with. But if it doesn't than I think that's an issue. I would also worry, a little bit, that even if it covers everybody we have a trade agreement with Ukraine, I don't think, is a WTO member and they're not a NATO member.

They are WTO? OK. So I worry, I would make sure that we want to capture all of the countries that we want to help and make sure they're not excluded as well.

It's the challenge with picking winners.

Senator MURKOWSKI. Madame Chairman, thank you. Again, I think that this has been very, very beneficial, very timely and thank each and every one of the witnesses, your leadership as well. Looking forward to working with you.

The CHAIR. Thank you. Meeting adjourned.

[Whereupon, at 12:16 p.m. the hearing was adjourned.]

APPENDIXES

Appendix I

Responses to Additional Questions

RESPONSES OF JAROSLAV NEVEROVIČ TO QUESTIONS FROM SENATOR LANDRIEU

Question 1. The focus of our hearing was on LNG exports and the US' role as a global energy power, but I believe we can export more than just LNG. We can also export our technical expertise, which is substantial, to help our allies develop their own resources. Louisiana, Oklahoma, Colorado and Texas, just to name a few, have world class energy service industries. Do you have any specific ideas about how their expertise may be better developed to assist other countries?

Answer. The U.S. can "export" a vision and share technological know-how in the LNG sector and unconventional oil & gas production with countries in Europe. Energy consumers in Eastern Europe are still locked not only in a technical lockout of gas supplies from one source, but also in a notion that there is no alternative to "pipelines", "Russian gas" and "Gazprom".

Message about shale gas and oil revolution, clean and environmentally production, liquefaction and transportability of LNG should be delivered to broader Eastern European constituencies. The U.S. could not only liberalize LNG export to Europe, but also share the notion that through technological advance and innovations more and more alternative gas and other energy resources will be available for "energy islands" like the Baltic States or other European countries.

More specifically that would assist Lithuania and other Russian-gas dependent countries in countering the Russian-inspired propaganda campaign to stop any local or alternative energy resource development in these countries that undermine Gazprom's market interests, but meet those countries' strategic energy independence goals. Support to those countries should be voiced by the U.S. Government and company officials at all levels and as frequently as possible.

Lithuania has good examples of the U.S. technical expertise in developing hydrocarbon resources and providing energy advisory services in nuclear energy, LNG terminal construction in our country. During the recent years Lithuania has been successfully cooperating with a number of the U.S. energy companies in implementing strategic energy projects—Fluor (Klaipeda LNG terminal), General Electric, Exelon (Visaginas Nuclear Power Plant), Science Applications International Corporation.

The U.S. expertise in utilization of municipal waste or biomass (wood, straw, short rotation coppice, etc.) for energy (electricity and heat) generation, exchange of know-how in technological solutions of utilization of municipal waste could also be useful for Lithuania as well as for other countries.

Question 2. What can the US do now to help our friends in Ukraine develop their own energy resources?

Answer. Being heavily dependent on gas imported from Russia (in 2010, 68 percent of gas came from Russia), Ukraine needs both short-term and long-term solutions. The U.S. administration and U.S. business could help Ukraine to diversify its imports and develop its own natural gas production capacity.

Firstly, in the short run, the EU and the U.S. could pull together their efforts to supply gas into the Ukrainian gas transmission system from Europe via Slovakia as well as fill Ukrainian underground gas storages with gas other than from Gazprom. We highly support efforts led by the U.S. diplomats and EU officials. We are hearing encouraging statements from the Slovakian leadership. Besides the diplomatic efforts, investments into infrastructure of reverse supplies and additional capacities of gas are necessary. At least 13 percent of annual Ukrainian gas needs could be imported from Europe via Slovakia, given that the price of gas is competitive and amounts are available. Therefore, more liberal gas exports from the U.S. to Europe definitely would make a change.

Secondly, in the long term, the U.S. and Europe (including private capital) could work together in helping Ukraine in 4 areas: 1) build its own LNG import facility on the shores of the Black Sea (as we have entered the final stage of completing our own LNG terminal in Klaipeda, our project management team is very well experienced on swift and "state of the art" project implementation and it can be used for similar purposes in Ukraine); 2) increasing natural gas production in Ukraine from conventional and unconventional gas fields, supporting Ukraine's switch from "net energy importer" to "net energy exporter" (it is expected that Ukraine can be rich of shale gas); 3) modernizing and jointly with Western investors exploiting Ukrainian gas transportation system (Ukraine has the biggest gas storage capacities in Europe); 4) substantially increasing energy efficiency in Ukraine (currently energy intensity in Ukraine is 11 times higher than the EU average). All these efforts will need long-term commitments from the U.S. and the EU, substantial financial support and technical expertise, but if successful, will transform the energy landscape in Ukraine.

Question 3. Also please outline what kind of investment from the U.S. you believe would make a significant impact in Ukraine?

Answer. The U.S. Government and businesses can work closely with the Ukrainian Government in creating favorable investment climate. This would attract more foreign investors in increasing gas and oil production in Ukraine, which has been falling from 68 bcm in 1975 to 20 bcm in recent years.

Question 4. Can you discuss what role the North American energy alliance of the United States, Mexico, and Canada, can play in helping not only Ukraine but the rest of our allies around the world?

Answer. Global gas market is only at creation stage. Global players like the U.S. and Canada could become global exporters of gas and substantially push forward the creation of a global gas market. Contemporary technologies are already enabling energy companies to transport gas at a relatively low cost. Energy islands like the Baltic States or other heavily dependent Eastern European countries like Ukraine would benefit greatly and immediately. Europe and the U.S. should act together and speedily.

Question 5a. I believe that a strong case has been made for the U.S. to have a measurable impact on the global LNG market. We must allow export terminals to enter the market quickly enough to seize a piece of the growing global demand for LNG. It would seem, then, accelerated approval for those projects most likely to be built would have the greatest positive impact on our allies and our most reliable trade partners-what is your opinion on:

Separating those projects that have spent considerable time and money to file with FERC into a separate approval queue?

Answer. Lithuania is currently 100 percent dependent on Russian gas and will start importing LNG as an alternative to pipeline gas from 2015 onwards. Adding extra export capacities to the global LNG market would directly or indirectly impact LNG importing countries such as Lithuania that are aiming to secure LNG supply under the current LNG market conditions of growing demand and limited supply.

Therefore, we consider increasing demand in LNG market as very important and we prefer this happening sooner rather than later.

Question 5b. Separating those projects under the jurisdiction of United States Maritime Administration (MARAD), which currently has jurisdiction over two projects, into a separate queue in order to better reflect their different approval process and timeline?

Answer. See the answer 5 (a) above.

RESPONSE OF JAROSLAV NEVEROVIČ TO QUESTION FROM SENATOR BARRASSO

Question 1. In your testimony, you discuss the Independence. You say that: "you cannot overstress the strategic importance of the LNG terminal to Lithuania." You explain that the Independence will be: "the ice-breaker for the region, helping to ensure an alternative gas supply and create a functioning gas market." Would you please expand upon your comments for the Committee?

Answer. The Baltic States and Finland are compared to an "energy island" in the context of the EU internal energy market due to the absence of gas interconnections with any other EU Member States (see the map* below) and a 100 percent dependency on gas supply from Russia when the EU average is around 25 percent.

---

*All maps have been retained in committee files.

This isolation and lack of gas pipeline interconnections with other EU Member States was largely determined by the historical circumstances of the Post—WWII period. This creates potential energy security threats thus leaving the Baltic States and Finland gas consumers and national economies vulnerable to gas supply interruptions and fluctuations of gas prices compared to countries with more diversified (better connected) or self-sufficient energy systems.

The Baltic States together with Finland have annual gas consumption of around 325 bcf (Lithuania alone—117 bcf) with a potential to grow. So far this whole demand is being covered by a single gas supplier—Gazprom. Due to the absence of competition in gas supply, the Eastern-Baltic region is paying one of the highest prices for gas among EU Member States. Lithuania, in fact, in the 2nd Q of 2013 was paying the highest price for natural gas among all EU Member States (around 14$/million Btu).

Even a small increase in the already high energy price creates a painful spill-over effect on Lithuania's economy, which is based on exports, by hindering the ability to compete in the EU and global markets. In this context, enhancement or assurance of energy security and development of competition through alternative gas supply sources are urgently needed.

Klaipeda LNG Terminal project in Lithuania is seen as the most effective way for creating an alternative source of natural gas supply, eliminating the dependence on the sole external gas supplier, providing coverage of emergency demand, creating conditions for national and regional gas markets, and enabling the country to access gas spot markets.

Lithuanian LNG terminal will have up to 141,2 bcf annual import capacity and that will be a key game changer for the three Baltic States with total annual gas consumption of 194,2 bcf.

The newly-built FSRU for the Lithuanian LNG terminal has been symbolically named "Independence". Although the primary goal of the Lithuanian LNG terminal is to satisfy national needs, the terminal will operate under the so called "third party access" regime, which means that our neighbors and partners will also have a possibility to use the spare terminal's capacity for their own needs. Klaipeda LNG Terminal will be the first large scale LNG terminal in the Baltic Sea with a capability to provide bunkering opportunities from all year round ice-free port. FSRU "Independence" will be "the ice-breaker" for the region, helping to ensure an alternative gas supply and create a functioning gas market.

———

RESPONSES OF EDWARD C. CHOW TO QUESTIONS FROM SENATOR LANDRIEU

Question 1. The focus of our hearing was on LNG exports and the US' role as a global energy power, but I believe we can export more than just LNG. We can also export our technical expertise, which is substantial, to help our allies develop their own resources. Louisiana, Oklahoma, Colorado and Texas, just to name a few, have world class energy service industries. Do you have any specific ideas about how their expertise may be better developed to assist other countries?

Answer. Ukraine has well-known geological potential to produce indigenous energy, including oil and gas. However, resource development and modernization of the energy sector have been blocked by pervasive corruption involving the highest levels of Ukrainian government which siphoned off billions of dollars every year since independence in 1991. This negatively affects equity investors as well as oilfield service and equipment suppliers. Until a new Ukrainian government commits to reform of the energy sector and actually implements concrete steps, outside assistance can make very little impact beyond bailing Ukraine out of an immediate crisis, only to have the same problem return a couple of years later as it has for more than two decades.

Question 2. What can the US do now to help our friends in Ukraine develop their own energy resources?

Answer. All Western assistance should be strictly conditional on real energy sector reform, with regular monitoring of the performance of the Ukrainian government by the donor community. This should apply to direct U.S. assistance, as well as those from international financial institutions such as the International Monetary Fund, World Bank, European Bank for Reconstruction and Development in which the U.S. holds major voting shares. Reform must start with pricing reform at both the burner-tip as well as the wellhead. Naftogaz, the Ukrainian national oil and gas company which is at the center of energy sector corruption, must be completely restructured and ultimately broken up and privatized. In order to do this in a proper and transparent way, Ukraine will need a lot of capacity building help including teams of technical, business, and regulatory experts. The U.S. must be prepared to do this if we are serious about helping Ukraine on energy.

Question 3. Also please outline what kind of investment from the U.S. you believe would make a significant impact in Ukraine?

Answer. Provision of aid without capacity building help and close supervision would be a total waste of taxpayers' money. Once the business climate is fundamentally improved, private-sector investments will flow to take advantage of the tremendous economic opportunities available in Ukraine, including in the energy sector.

Question 4. Can you discuss what role the North American energy alliance of the United States, Mexico, and Canada, can play in helping not only Ukraine but the rest of our allies around the world?

Answer. Both the U.S. and Canada possess the capability, including by independent producers and service providers, which can benefit Ukraine and other Central and Eastern European countries on energy innovation, such as shale gas and tight oil. Mexico is a country which is finally opening up its oil and gas sector to private investment as part of an overall modernization program for its economy in spite decades of political roadblocks. It offers an example Ukraine should follow.

Question 5. I believe that a strong case has been made for the U.S. to have a measurable impact on the global LNG market. We must allow export terminals to enter the market quickly enough to seize a piece of the growing global demand for LNG. It would seem, then, accelerated approval for those projects most likely to be built would have the greatest positive impact on our allies and our most reliable trade partners-what is your opinion on:

a. Separating those projects that have spent considerable time and money to file with FERC into a separate approval queue?

b. Separating those projects under the jurisdiction of United States Maritime Administration (MARAD), which currently has jurisdiction over two projects, into a separate queue in order to better reflect their different approval process and timeline?

Answer. A LNG export terminal project takes 3 to 5 years to finish from conception to completion. The DOE-approval is just the initial step in that process. There are good domestic economic reasons to remove restrictions from energy trade which were formulated decades ago in a much different environment. However, American LNG is unlikely to have much impact on the global market in the short to medium term.

Question 6. What, in your opinion, is the likelihood that Russia will continue to raise prices of its natural gas exports?

Answer. Russia has actually provided more contract flexibility and lowered its exported gas prices in the last couple of years to all its major West European customers in order to meet market prices and protect market share. As a result, West European LNG import terminals are severely underutilized. Russia has not provided similar contract flexibility and pricing discounts to Central and East European customers because they have not developed alternative sources of gas imports and Russia is often their only supplier.

Question 7. What other ways does Russia have to raise revenue?

Answer. Actually natural gas contributes a much smaller portion of Russia's export earnings and budget revenue than oil, which is ten times more important. Russia is propped up economically by historically high global oil prices. Gas has a bigger impact politically. Together oil and gas represent more than 50 percent of Russia's federal budget and 70 percent of export earnings.

RESPONSES OF EDWARD C. CHOW TO QUESTIONS FROM SENATOR MURKOWSKI

Question 8. Is the deployment of floating LNG facilities to the Black Sea a practical way of delivering gas to Ukraine?

Answer. No, not in the short to medium term and not without structural reform of Ukraine's gas market. Importing LNG will certainly be more expensive than increasing domestic gas production and pipeline imports. A LNG import terminal for Ukraine would not be economically viable and will be difficult to finance. Turkish objection over LNG transit via the Bosphorus is another practical obstacle.

Question 9. In your opinion, are there reasons for expediting the build-out of U.S. liquefaction capacity that are separate from the situation in Ukraine?

Answer. Yes, as I stated in my testimony, there are ample domestic economic reasons to revisit the policy of restricting U.S. gas and crude oil exports. With gas, it has to do with ensuring investment conditions exist to sustain shale gas production at a level that is beneficial to domestic producers as well as to long-term consumers of gas. With crude oil, it has to do with maintaining the competitive advantage of our highly-sophisticated refineries to process cheaper, heavy and sour, imported crudes while gaining maximum economic benefits for the country by exporting light, sweet crudes.

RESPONSES OF DAVID MONTGOMERY TO QUESTIONS FROM SENATOR LANDRIEU

Question 1. The focus of our hearing was on LNG exports and the US' role as a global energy power, but I believe we can export more than just LNG. We can also export our technical expertise, which is substantial, to help our allies develop their own resources. Louisiana, Oklahoma, Colorado and Texas, just to name a few, have world class energy service industries. Do you have any specific ideas about how their expertise may be better developed to assist other countries?

Answer. I believe oil and gas E&P companies and oil field service companies are ready to move anywhere in the world where there is a demand for their services. For them to do so in particular countries requires manageable levels of corruption, sound geology, property rights that favor development, fair taxation, and a secure investment climate. Oil service companies have been able to work in many dangerous and risky countries. To expand those opportunities the best role for the U.S. government is to aid in resolving conflict situations and provide incentives for institutional change toward a more favorable investment climate.

Question 2. What can the U.S. do now to help our friends in Ukraine develop their own energy resources?

Answer. In previous work (available at http://www.iccfglobal.org/pdf/APPsummary.pdf), I have studied the role of institutional reform and strategies to overcome barriers that are common across developing countries (including Ukraine in this case) in a different context (climate and economic growth nexus), never the less the message still remains the same. To develop efficient market in Ukraine there are certain fundamental reforms that are necessary and my research in the past has highlighted that.

The critical enabling actions need to be taken by the Ukraine government. Under the previous regime, the Ukraine was rated as one of the most corrupt countries in the world. This has to change before there can be an investment climate favorable to energy development. Providing whatever aid the Ukraine can use to root out corruption in its bureaucracy and establish open procedures for governance of energy activities is probably the best direct action we could take now. But the U.S. could help Ukraine indirectly if it were to remove barriers to exporting energy of all kinds. U.S. natural gas supplies won't make a big impact in the near-term, but lifting the crude oil export ban could affect the world oil market and lessen Russia's grip.

Question 3. Also please outline what kind of investment from the U.S. you believe would make a significant impact in Ukraine?

Answer. If the new government can suppress corruption and create a more open economy, investment will flow into development of its energy resources with no other action by the U.S. government. As a response to Russian aggression, the U.S. could acquire floating LNG regasification barges for use by Ukraine and grant emergency clearance for floating liquefaction plants to begin operation off the U.S. Gulf Coast. The purpose of this short run strategy would be to break Russia's ability to extort higher prices for natural gas. This would have to be done for strategic reasons, since it likely would not provide an economic return. This step could be part of a broader strategy to signal to the world that the U.S. is open to exporting its gas, and therefore if Russia wants to maintain sales it will have to give Ukraine more favorable terms when it renegotiates its long-term gas contracts.

Question 4. Can you discuss what role the North American energy alliance of the United States, Mexico, and Canada, can play in helping not only Ukraine but the rest of our allies around the world?

Answer. Maximizing production and freeing up exports will have a long term effect of reducing Russia's energy export revenues, economic power, and ability to reconquer the former Soviet Republics and intimidate Eastern Europe. Approval of the Keystone pipeline and removing the crude oil export ban would be two concrete actions that would free up exports.

Question 5. I believe that a strong case has been made for the U.S. to have a measurable impact on the global LNG market. We must allow export terminals to enter the market quickly enough to seize a piece of the growing global demand for LNG. It would seem, then, accelerated approval for those projects most likely to be built would have the greatest positive impact on our allies and our most reliable trade partners-what is your opinion on:

64

5a. Separating those projects that have spent considerable time and money to file with FERC into a separate approval queue?

5b. Separating those projects under the jurisdiction of United States Maritime Administration (MARAD), which currently has jurisdiction over two projects, into a separate queue in order to better reflect their different approval process and timeline?

Answer. Yes, both would speed up the process. Neither would constitute a complete signal of our willingness to be an effective potential competitor to Russia because neither eliminates the possibility that politics could change and place a limit on exports sufficiently low to prevent them from reducing Russia's market share and/or price. A much stronger signal would be sent by the declaration that all LNG exports are in the public interest.

Question 6a. You make the case in your study that exports will drive additional production levels, and that additional production will fill a majority of the increased demand for natural gas in the U.S. associated with export. What is your estimate of the employment impact of this increased production.

Could you explain the scale of the impact that unconstrained export would have on the most gas intensive manufacturing sectors? Specifically, why ethylene and polyethylene industries are predicted to grow even in the case of unconstrained exports?

Answer. There clearly will be increased employment in natural gas production as a result of LNG exports, since natural gas production will increase by almost the amount of exports. We did not make a separate calculation of increased employment in natural gas exploration and production attributable to LNG exports in our updated study.

LNG exports would have very little effect on even the most gas intensive manufacturing sectors, because LNG exports cannot change U.S. natural gas prices nearly enough to erase the built in advantage of domestic manufacturers over their rivals in countries that import natural gas. Even with the maximum LNG exports projected in our scenarios, The price of natural gas for U.S. manufacturers will remain about half the natural gas prices faced in countries that import LNG. This is because the cost of liquefying, transporting and regasifying LNG from the U.S. to the most attractive importing region is approximately equal to the wellhead price of natural gas in the U.S. (*See Exhibit). 1 Adding this cost to the wellhead price in the U.S. implies that Asian manufacturers will continue to pay at least twice as much for natural gas as U.S. manufacturers.

The impacts of LNG exports on natural gas prices in the U.S. are likely to be modest, and in no case do they come close to the differential between U.S. natural gas prices and those paid by rivals to U.S. manufacturing in other countries. Exhibit 2 below shows that when we base the international demand for LNG on EIA's reference case from the most recent International Energy Outlook (indicated by red icons in the Exhibit), we find that the increase in natural gas prices is about 25 cents per Mcf with EIA Reference Case assumptions about U.S. oil and gas supply from AEO2013. The largest price impact attributable to LNG exports is about $1.00 per Mcf in a case that is constructed to incorporate a very unlikely level of global demand for U.S. LNG. Even this highly unlikely impact would not come close to closing the cost advantage for U.S. manufacturing of about $6.00 per Mcf.

It is incorrect to label the $.75 to $1.06 maximum price impacts seen in Exhibit 3 as price forecasts. They occur in cases that were constructed as stress tests, to determine impacts on the U.S. economy if global natural gas markets were severely disrupted by widespread and permanent shutdown of nuclear power and cancellation of even currently planned LNG export projects in major exporting countries. Leaving aside questions of whether global demand for LNG could remain as high as projected at these prices, it is highly likely that the high global natural gas prices projected in the supply and demand shock cases would lead to appearance of other projects and supplies to get around the assumed constraints on global production. Even in these cases, LNG exports provide net benefits to the U.S. and the net benefits of LNG exports are greatest with no limits placed on those exports.

Exhibit 3[1] displays global supply curves for ethylene, a major chemical product and export, before and after the shale revolution. The curve labeled 2005 shows the relative position of the U.S. before the shale revolution. At that time, the U.S. was the highest cost producer and highly vulnerable to expanded production in other regions. The shale revolution reversed all that, and put the U.S. in a virtual tie with the Middle East as the lowest cost producer of ethylene. Moreover, the next lowest

---

* All exhibits have been retained in committee files.

[1] American Chemistry Council, Shale Gas, Competitiveness, and New US Chemical Industry Investment: An Analysis Based on Announced Projects, May 2013, p. 21

65

cost producer, China, has a cost at least 50 cents per pound greater than the U.S. cost of manufacturing ethylene. Western Europe and Japan, the highest cost producers and therefore relevant competitors to the U.S., have costs 90 cents to $1.00 per pound greater than the U.S.

We calculated the amount that even the highly unlikely maximum price increase of $1 per Mcf would make in the cost of producing ethylene. It amounts to about 5 cents per pound, or about 5 percent—10 percent of the current cost advantage that the U.S. has over rivals in countries that import natural gas.

With this wide a cost advantage, LNG exports do not threaten the competitive position of U.S. manufacturing. Moreover, ethylene and polyethylene benefit from the excess supply of its specific feedstock, ethane, that will grow with increased exports. Ethane used to sell for about $2 per Mcf more than pipeline quality natural gas, but that has changed because shale formations produce much wetter gas than conventional formations. Ethane is a large component of this wetter gas, and the ratio of ethane to dry gas production exceeds the level that is allowed to be shipped in interstate pipelines due to safety risks. This has stranded ethane, driving its price down to rough parity with natural gas. Producing more natural gas for export will increase the amount of stranded ethane, and likely keep its price depressed from historical levels for some time. This is one of the primary reasons that ethylene and polyethylene production in the U.S. increase as LNG exports increase.

RESPONSES OF DAVID MONTGOMERY TO QUESTIONS FROM SENATOR MURKOWSKI

Question 1. U.S. natural gas exports via pipeline are at record high levels. Have you observed any detrimental impact on the U.S. economy, either in terms of supply availability or price volatility? Would you expect liquefied natural gas exports to be any different?

Answer. No. From an economic perspective LNG exports and pipeline exports are the same. They involve investment in infrastructure, open markets to goods (natural gas) where we enjoy a global competitive advantage, and improve our balance of payments. Regarding price volatility, short-term price upsets like those experienced this winter will not go away if we prohibit exports. These rapid changes in price are caused by local supply/demand factors. More storage would alleviate price spikes, but storage is expensive and may not be economic on a long term basis.

Exports of any kind add to natural gas infrastructure and have created a larger and better connected market that is able to move natural gas to wherever increased demand exists. This is also true of LNG exports, which could lead to creation of additional natural gas infrastructure in certain regions, which has the potential to alleviate some existing bottlenecks, increase supply availability and reduce price volatility. For example, if additional pipeline capacity had been built to move natural gas through New England to Atlantic LNG export terminals, that gas could have been bid away from exports and added to New England supply during the price spikes that developed last winter. Moreover, LNG exports would likely be served by increased production from shale gas formations, these sources are in locations where they are not as vulnerable to the extreme weather events that threaten Gulf Coast production. This increase in geographical diversity will reduce the impact of weather related events on natural gas prices.

Question 2. How sensitive is your analysis to unexpected domestic consumption of natural gas? In other words, if the industrial, transportation, or electricity sectors end up consuming more than forecasted, would that force a reappraisal of your views on LNG exports?

Answer. No. It would lead to a different forecast of exports, but would not change my view that market-determined levels of exports provide the largest economic benefits whatever the level of consumption. Higher levels of demand than contained in our scenarios would be accompanied by increased supply; if that led to upward pressure on prices, LNG exports would expand less rapidly because the U.S. would be a less competitive supplier in global markets. Thus higher demand in the U.S. could lead to higher prices than in scenarios with lower demand, but those price increases would be ameliorated by lower export levels. I am confident that it would remain true that a policy of placing no limits on exports would even in these cases provide larger benefits than any restrictive policy. My opinion is based on our examination of scenarios in which we did assume reference levels of supply and higher growth in demand. In none of these alternative high demand baselines did domestic natural gas prices rise as high as they did in the low supply cases; therefore the impacts of LNG exports in high demand cases would fall within the range of cases we did examine.

Question 3. How real is the possibility that LNG exports would divert domestic gas away from domestic consumers?

Answer. Our analysis shows that most LNG exported from the U.S. will come from increased production, and very little will be diverted from domestic customers. This is simply a matter of the relatively flat supply curve for shale gas that is found by most independent studies, and the high value in use of natural gas in U.S. manufacturing.

The chart below (Exhibit 1) shows the sources from which exports are drawn in a relatively high export case, our reference case with unconstrained exports and a global demand shock. Increases in natural gas production equal about 80 percent of the volume exported plus losses and consumption in liquefaction. The largest demand reduction occurs in the electric power sector, where renewables and, to the extent allowable under EPA rules, coal substitute for natural gas. Changes in residential, transportation and energy-intensive manufacturing uses of natural gas are negligible compared to the level of exports.

Question 4. How real is the possibility that LNG exports would harm other sectors of the U.S. economy by raising natural gas prices domestically and/or becoming linked with worldwide energy markets? Is "parity" a threat?

Answer. LNG exports are not a threat to other sectors of the U.S. economy. LNG exports are unlikely to affect U.S. natural gas prices nearly enough to erase the built in advantage of domestic manufacturers over their rivals in countries that import natural gas. Even with the maximum LNG exports projected in our scenarios, The price of natural gas for U.S. manufacturers will remain about half the natural gas prices faced in countries that import LNG. This is because the cost of liquefying, transporting and regasifying LNG from the U.S. to the most attractive importing region is approximately equal to the wellhead price of natural gas in the U.S. (See Exhibit 2). Adding this cost to the wellhead price in the U.S. implies that Asian manufacturers will continue to pay at least twice as much for natural gas as U.S. manufacturers.

The impacts of LNG exports on natural gas prices in the U.S. are likely to be modest, and in no case do they come close to the differential between U.S. natural gas prices and those paid by rivals to U.S. manufacturing in other countries. Exhibit 3 below shows that when we base the international demand for LNG on EIA's reference case from the most recent International Energy Outlook (indicated by red icons in the Exhibit), we find that the increase in natural gas prices is about 25 cents per Mcf with EIA Reference Case assumptions about U.S. oil and gas supply from AEO2013. The largest price impact attributable to LNG exports is about $1.00 per Mcf in a case that is constructed to incorporate a very unlikely level of global demand for U.S. LNG. Even this highly unlikely impact would not come close to closing the cost advantage for U.S. manufacturing of about $6.00 per Mcf.

It is incorrect to label the $.75 to $1.06 maximum price impacts seen in Exhibit 3 as price forecasts. They occur in cases that were constructed as stress tests, to determine impacts on the U.S. economy if global natural gas markets were severely disrupted by widespread and permanent shutdown of nuclear power and cancellation of even currently planned LNG export projects in major exporting countries. Leaving aside questions of whether global demand for LNG could remain as high as projected at these prices, it is highly likely that the high global natural gas prices projected in the supply and demand shock cases would lead to appearance of other projects and supplies to get around the assumed constraints on global production. Even in these cases, LNG exports provide net benefits to the U.S. and the net benefits of LNG exports are greatest with no limits placed on those exports.

Exhibit 4[2] displays global supply curves for ethylene, a major chemical product and export, before and after the shale revolution. The curve labeled 2005 shows the relative position of the U.S. before the shale revolution. At that time, the U.S. was the highest cost producer and highly vulnerable to expanded production in other regions. The shale revolution reversed all that, and put the U.S. in a virtual tie with the Middle East as the lowest cost producer of ethylene. Moreover, the next lowest cost producer, China, has a cost at least 50 cents per pound greater than the U.S. cost of manufacturing ethylene. Western Europe and Japan, the highest cost producers and therefore relevant competitors to the U.S., have costs 90 cents to $1.00 per pound greater than the U.S.

We calculated the amount that even the highly unlikely maximum price increase of $1 per Mcf would make in the cost of producing ethylene. It amounts to about 5 cents per pound, or about 5 percent—10 percent of the current cost advantage that the U.S. has over rivals in countries that import natural gas.

With this wide a cost advantage, LNG exports do not threaten the competitive position of U.S. manufacturing. Moreover, ethylene in particular benefits from the ex-

---

[2] American Chemistry Council, Shale Gas, Competitiveness, and New US Chemical Indstry Investment: An Analysis Based on Announced Projects, May 2013, p. 21

cess supply of its specific feedstock, ethane, that will grow with increased exports. Ethane used to sell for about $2 per Mcf more than pipeline quality natural gas, but that has changed because shale formations produce much wetter gas than conventional formations. Ethane is a large component of this wetter gas, and the ratio of ethane to dry gas production exceeds the level that is allowed to be shipped in interstate pipelines due to safety risks. This has stranded ethane, driving its price down to rough parity with natural gas. Producing more natural gas for export will increase the amount of stranded ethane, and likely keep its price depressed from historical levels for some time. This will be a further benefit to U.S. chemicals producers from LNG exports that we did not include in our calculations.

Question 5. Please discuss the differences between the NERA analysis and the Charles River Associates' report on the same subject. Where do you diverge on price impact, reference cast forecasts, and other important areas?

Answer. There is almost no relevant point of comparison between the statements found in CRA's report and NERA's analysis of the impact of LNG exports.

1. CRA does not discuss the impact of LNG exports on prices, but rather compares current prices to its own forecast of future prices. Most of the increase in prices forecasted by CRA occurs in their reference case, and LNG exports have no greater impact on prices than in our study. The statement in their report that LNG exports will make prices nearly triple is grossly misleading. CRA makes that happen by choosing to label as a "reference case" a forecast that is at or above just about every other independent production of natural gas prices with continued production of shale gas.

2. NERA did not make a "reference case forecast" as claimed by CRA; rather, we developed scenarios based on EIA's high oil and gas resource, reference, and low oil and gas resource cases from AEO2013. Both EIA and NERA recognize that there is great uncertainty about future natural gas prices, and that any specific forecast has only a slim chance of turning out to be correct. Therefore, we use a scenario approach and ask whether the consequences of a policy change, such as removing limits on LNG exports, are similar across all scenarios.[3] We find that in all the scenarios, unlimited LNG exports provide greater economic benefits than any lesser level constrained by DOE, U.S. consumers are not "deprived" of gas by exports, and U.S. natural gas prices never rise to oil parity levels or to levels seen in gas importing countries. For what it is worth, even CRA's price forecasts fall within the range of the scenarios we considered, and therefore their efforts to create an issue out of forecasts are pointless.

3. CRA does no integrated economic analysis of the impacts of LNG exports on energy supply and demand and the overall economy. Instead, CRA makes a series of calculations unrelated to the actual effects of exports on the economy, and uses these to conjure up images of disaster. Their images of disaster arise from three fundamental errors:

a. No analysis of global supply and demand to determine whether any importer would be willing to buy the amount of LNG exports claimed by CRA at the prices calculated by CRA

b. The false assumption that there will be no response of domestic gas production to LNG export demand, creating the false dichotomy of gas going either to manufacturing or to exports

c. Misuse of input-output data to support the impossible conclusion that more GDP will be created if the government rather than the market allocates energy, and does so in a manner that gives the largest allocation to those industries that use the least amount of energy relative to their cost of production.

d. Failure to compare current data on the relative cost of chemical production in the U.S. to costs in other countries. As shown in Exhibit 4, U.S. producers are now able to produce basic chemicals like ethylene at cost far below those of global competitors. There has been a surge of investment in capacity for producing ethylene in the U.S. since natural gas prices fell. According to the ACC, "the mix of projects announced thus far has been heavily slanted toward bulk petrochemicals, mainly steam crackers for ethylene . . . "[4] and these are not

---

[3] I have written previously on the topic of the problems of forecasting natural gas prices and the need for scenario analysis for robust decisions (see http://www.regulations.gov/#!documentDetail;D=EPA-HQ-OAR-2011-0660-9966) and our approach to scenario analysis is consistent with those opinions.

[4] American Chemistry Council, Shale Gas, Competitiveness, and New US Chemical Industry Investment: An Analysis Based on Announced Projects, May 2013, p. 25

in any way at risk from LNG exports, which at most could erode 5—10 percent of U.S. manufacturers cost advantage. Thus CRA's dire warnings of the loss of nearly $100 billion in chemical investment are a fiction.

Several absurd conclusions follow from the claims that CRA makes about the benefits of allocating natural gas to manufacturing and away from exports.

1. CRA assumes that there is an infinite supply of capital and labor, so that the additional amount of labor and capital needed to turn 1 Bcf of natural gas into manufactured products does not have to be taken away from any other productive enterprise (no opportunity cost for capital and labor). At the same time, CRA assumes that there is a fixed supply of natural gas, and that no matter how much capital and labor is added, it is impossible to produce any larger quantity. These are the only circumstances in which their hypothetical comparison of using 1 Bcf in manufacturing versus exporting 1 Bcf could have any relevance in the real world.

2. The recommendation based on this irrelevant calculation that exports of natural gas should be limited does not go far enough. Value added is nothing more or less than payments to labor and capital made out of the revenue of an industry. CRA calculates the ratio of value added to natural gas used in manufacturing and the ratio of value added to natural gas used for exports.

a. The ratios their argument rests on are not comparable. CRA calculates the ratio of value added to natural gas inputs for manufacturing and natural gas outputs for natural gas production. This is foolish. A consistent definition for NAICS 211, natural gas (and oil) production, would calculate the ratio of value added in NAICS 211 to the use of natural gas as an input to natural gas production. This ratio is in fact very high—around 98 percent. [If we look at natural gas production and export as an integrated operation, we see that there is very little natural gas used as an input to production of natural gas. Thus on CRA's argument, we should be putting more resources into natural gas exports in order to make production as high as possible.

b. CRA claims that natural gas should be allocated to chemical production rather than exports because there is more value added in chemical production than in exports. But CRA stops too soon. Value added per Bcf of natural gas use in chemicals is greater than in manufacturing as a whole, and in manufacturing as a whole, less than in services. Therefore, if CRA is correct about how to maximize GDP, we should first stop exporting any chemicals, so as to make the natural gas embodied in those chemicals available to the rest of manufacturing. But then we should go further and kill off the manufacturing renaissance itself, which is taking gas away from the service sector that has even higher value added per Btu of gas used.

c. A moment's reflection on these absurd results would have revealed how foolish CRA's argument for limiting exports really is. There is not a fixed supply of natural gas, nor an infinite supply of capital and labor. Making it the overriding goal of economic policy to expand the industries that have the highest value added per Bcf of natural gas used leads to obviously undesirable outcomes.

d. Thus, CRA has added nothing to the rent-seeking claim of chemical manufacturers that government should favor them by reducing their cost of production, and theirs alone, by preventing suppliers of their inputs from selling them to others. The logic of their argument should have forced CRA to conclude that the industry with the value added per Bcf of gas input should be allocated all the natural gas we produce. Likewise, the logic of the Dow claim could also be adopted by U.S. users of polyethylene and other bulk chemicals, who could equally well argue to prevent exports of bulk chemicals because there is more value added in manufacturing plastic components and finished goods from polyethylene than in exporting it.

NERA finds that there is no conflict between exporting natural gas and using it at home, except at the level of rent-seeking and attempts to enhance profits through favoritism by regulators. In a market with unrestricted natural gas and chemical exports, U.S. chemical producers would be able to purchase all the natural gas feedstocks they can profitably use. U.S. manufacturers would be able to choose between obtaining chemicals from U.S. or foreign producers depending on price, and would largely find that U.S. chemical producers could give a better deal because even with unlimited exports their natural gas costs would be far below competitors in importing countries. Natural gas producers would supply enough gas to satisfy export demand and all the gas that domestic consumers want to buy. The result is a higher level of GDP than could be achieved through any combination of restrictions on exports at any level.

Question 6. What does economic history tell us, if anything, about the real world consequences of government policies that constrain exports of energy (or other analogous commodities)?

Answer. The policy of constraining commodity exports in order to subsidize domestic processing and manufacturing industries has been uniformly rejected in the literature of economic development.[5]

Ghana provides a good example of the consequences of policies intended to shift income from producers of basic commodities to industries that use those products to create more value added. A government dominated by elites with an economic interest in development of industry adopted policies to keep prices of agricultural products low. These price controls made exports a much more attractive outlet for agricultural commodities, and to prevent this the government established marketing boards with exclusive rights to buy commodities from farmers and resell them. The outcome of depressed prices to farmers, contraction of a previously successful agricultural sector, and no success in creating sustainable industries with subsidies.[6]

Question 7. Do exports of "finished products" add to GDP more than exports of so-called "raw materials"? Should one category be more restricted than the other, or restricted at all?

Answer. No. The market test is which category of exports obtains the most revenue per dollar of resources devoted. Value added is a cost, not a benefit, as it is the payment made for labor and for capital services. If an hour of labor and 1 million of capital are put to work in one industry, they are no longer available for another. So the idea is to get as much revenue as possible for the capital and labor employed, not to employ as much labor and capital as possible per dollar of revenue.

The contention that there is a choice is also false. There is enough gas for both.

Question 8. Can U.S. LNG exports solely to Asia still affect the Europe-Russia dynamic in any meaningful way?

Answer. Yes. The LNG market is a global market so the more LNG supplies that are added to the market the more the world price of gas will be driven down . By virtue of there being a world gas market, any supplies that the U.S. sends to Asia will eventually back out some of the suppliers to Europe since the suppliers that lose market share in Asia because of being displaced by the U.S. will likely shift some of their supplies to Europe thus possibly displacing some Russian supplies and certainly lowering the price of gas in Europe. Already see it in U.S. demand for LNG imports disappearing, reducing Russian exports and prices. Now if the U.S. becomes a significant exporter, it will increase the pressure on Russia to lower its prices. Doesn't matter where our gas goes, it will send gas to Europe by displacement

Question 9. When did NERA submit a complete draft of its 2012 LNG study to the Department of Energy? Were substantive edits required?

Answer. NERA delivered a final complete draft of its report to DOE on July 11, 2012. No substantive edits were requested, and except for changing the date and removing the "draft" labels, the identical report was released by DOE in December 2012.

RESPONSE OF DAVID MONTGOMERY TO QUESTION FROM SENATOR CANTWELL

Question 1. NERA's statistics and analysis of the economic impacts of liquefied natural gas exports differ quite a bit from statistics and analysis from some other institutions that are studying natural gas export issues, such as Charles River Associates and Purdue University. Could you please explain the differences between Purdue University, Charles River Associates and NERA data and analysis?

Answer. There is almost no relevant point of comparison between the statements found in CRA's report and NERA's analysis of the impact of LNG exports. CRA does not

1. CRA does not discuss the impact of LNG exports on prices, but rather compares current prices to its own forecast of future prices. Most of the increase in prices forecasted by CRA occurs in their reference case, and LNG exports have no greater impact on prices than in our study. The statement in their report that LNG exports will make prices nearly triple is grossly misleading. CRA makes that happen by choosing to label as a "reference case" a forecast that is at or above just about every other independent production of natural gas prices with continued production of shale gas.

---

[5] See, for example, Angus Deaton, Commodity prices and growth in Africa, Journal of Economic Perspectives—Volume 13, Number 3—Summer 1999—Pages 23–40
[6] Robert Bates, Markets and states in tropical Africa: the political basis of agricultural policies, Univ of California Press, 1981

2. NERA did not make a "reference case forecast" as claimed by CRA; rather, we developed scenarios based on EIA's high oil and gas resource, reference, and low oil and gas resource cases from AEO2013. Both EIA and NERA recognize that there is great uncertainty about future natural gas prices, and that any specific forecast has only a slim chance of turning out to be correct. Therefore, we use a scenario approach and ask whether the consequences of a policy change, such as removing limits on LNG exports, are similar across all scenarios.[7] We find that in all the scenarios, unlimited LNG exports provide greater economic benefits than any lesser level constrained by DOE, U.S. consumers are not "deprived" of gas by exports, and U.S. natural gas prices never rise to oil parity levels or to levels seen in gas importing countries. For what it is worth, even CRA's price forecasts fall within the range of the scenarios we considered, and therefore their efforts to create an issue out of forecasts are pointless.

3. CRA does no integrated economic analysis of the impacts of LNG exports on energy supply and demand and the overall economy. Instead, CRA makes a series of calculations unrelated to the actual effects of exports on the economy, cherrypicks data to create an unrealistically gloomy picture of the vulnerability of chemicals production to foreign competition, and uses these to conjure up images of disaster. Their images of disaster arise from four fundamental errors:

a. No analysis of global supply and demand to determine whether any importer would be willing to buy the amount of LNG exports claimed by CRA at the prices calculated by CRA

b. The false assumption that there will be no response of domestic gas production to LNG export demand, creating the false dichotomy of gas going either to manufacturing or to exports

c. Misuse of input-output data to support the impossible conclusion that more GDP will be created if the government rather than the market allocates energy, and does so in a manner that gives the largest allocation to those industries that use the least amount of energy relative to their cost of production.

d. Failure to compare current data on the relative cost of chemical production in the U.S. to costs in other countries. As shown in Exhibit 4, U.S. producers are now able to produce basic chemicals like ethylene at cost far below those of global competitors. There has been a surge of investment in capacity for producing ethylene in the U.S. since natural gas prices fell. According to the ACC, "the mix of projects announced thus far has been heavily slanted toward bulk petrochemicals, mainly steam crackers for ethylene . . . "[8] and these are not in any way at risk from LNG exports, which at most could erode 5—10 percent of U.S. manufacturers cost advantage. Thus CRA's dire warnings of the loss of nearly $100 billion in chemical investment are a fiction.

Several absurd conclusions follow from the claims that CRA makes about the benefits of allocating natural gas to manufacturing and away from exports.

1. CRA assumes that there is an infinite supply of capital and labor, so that the additional amount of labor and capital needed to turn 1 Bcf of natural gas into manufactured products does not have to be taken away from any other productive enterprise (no opportunity cost for capital and labor). At the same time, CRA assumes that there is a fixed supply of natural gas, and that no matter how much capital and labor is added, it is impossible to produce any larger quantity. These are the only circumstances in which their hypothetical comparison of using 1 Bcf in manufacturing versus exporting 1 Bcf could have any relevance in the real world.

2. The recommendation based on this irrelevant calculation that exports of natural gas should be limited does not go far enough. Value added is nothing more or less than payments to labor and capital made out of the revenue of an industry. CRA calculates the ratio of value added to natural gas used in manufacturing and the ratio of value added to natural gas used for exports.

a. The ratios their argument rests on are not comparable. CRA calculates the ratio of value added to natural gas inputs for manufacturing and natural gas outputs for natural gas production. This is foolish. A consistent definition for NAICS 211, natural gas (and oil) production, would calculate the ratio of value added in NAICS 211 to the use of natural gas as an input to natural gas pro-

[7] I have written previously on the topic of the problems of forecasting natural gas prices and the need for scenario analysis for robust decisions (see http://www.regulations.gov/#!documentDetail;D=EPA-HQ-OAR-2011-0660-9966) and our approach to scenario analysis is consistent with those opinions.
[8] American Chemistry Council, Shale Gas, Competitiveness, and New US Chemical Industry Investment: An Analysis Based on Announced Projects, May 2013, p. 25

duction. This ratio is in fact very high—around 98 percent. [If we look at natural gas production and export as an integrated operation, we see that there is very little natural gas used as an input to production of natural gas. Thus on CRA's argument, we should be putting more resources into natural gas exports in order to make production as high as possible.

b. CRA claims that natural gas should be allocated to chemical production rather than exports because there is more value added in chemical production than in exports. But CRA stops too soon. Value added per Bcf of natural gas use in chemicals is greater than in manufacturing as a whole, and in manufacturing as a whole, less than in services. Therefore, if CRA is correct about how to maximize GDP, we should first stop exporting any chemicals, so as to make the natural gas embodied in those chemicals available to the rest of manufacturing. But then we should go further and kill off the manufacturing renaissance itself, which is taking gas away from the service sector that has even higher value added per Btu of gas used.

c. A moment's reflection on these absurd results would have revealed how foolish CRA's argument for limiting exports really is. There is not a fixed supply of natural gas, nor an infinite supply of capital and labor. Making it the overriding goal of economic policy to expand the industries that have the highest value added per Bcf of natural gas used leads to obviously undesirable outcomes.

d. Thus, CRA has added nothing to the rent-seeking claim of chemical manufacturers that government should favor them by reducing their cost of production, and theirs alone, by preventing suppliers of their inputs from selling them to others. The logic of their argument should have forced CRA to conclude that the industry with the value added per Bcf of gas input should be allocated all the natural gas we produce. Likewise, the logic of the Dow claim could also be adopted by U.S. users of polyethylene and other bulk chemicals, who could equally well argue to prevent exports of bulk chemicals because there is more value added in manufacturing plastic components and finished goods from polyethylene than in exporting it.

As to the Purdue analysis, we have reviewed in detail their published articles and the model code that they have made available. The model that they use to evaluate impacts of LNG exports does not appear to include a complete accounting of the costs and benefits of exports. Costs are fully represented, but we are unable to find anywhere in their model code a term that represents the benefits of LNG exports as the difference between the cost of producing the incremental production that supports exports and the revenues received for those exports. When the market determines supply and demand for exports, as it would if exports are not limited, that difference must be positive. When exports are restricted, the difference is still positive but smaller. In other words, the revenues from selling a quantity of natural gas overseas must exceed the cost of producing it or no one would be willing to sell. This component of the gain from trade appears to be missing from Purdue's calculation of GDP impacts.

————

RESPONSES OF DAVID L. GOLDWYN TO QUESTIONS FROM SENATOR LANDRIEU

Question 1. The focus of our hearing was on LNG exports and the US' role as a global energy power, but I believe we can export more than just LNG. We can also export our technical expertise, which is substantial, to help our allies develop their own resources. Louisiana, Oklahoma, Colorado and Texas, just to name a few, have world-class energy service industries. Do you have any specific ideas about how their expertise may be better developed to assist other countries?

Answer. The U.S. oil and gas industry is world-class, and has extensive experience with energy development in the U.S. and abroad. U.S. companies routinely bid on and develop resources abroad, and U.S. based service companies provide foreign oil companies (be they national oil companies or privately-held companies) with experienced labor and cutting edge technologies. The industry is already active abroad in developing indigenous supplies of oil and gas, including shale and other unconventionals, in ways that are beneficial to both the host companies and the companies themselves. Greater involvement of U.S. industry in oil and gas development abroad will raise the likelihood that indigenous resource development will be successful, and that the advanced technologies and best practices that have been perfected over time in the U.S. will be safely and efficiently implemented abroad. Industry can also help by participating in and/or helping to shape vocational education programs to help train skilled labor abroad, another effort that benefits the host government, local communities and U.S. companies that may later need that skilled labor to complete its projects in that country.

Industry can also assist by encouraging foreign nations interested in shale oil and gas development to participate in the Unconventional Gas Technical Engagement Program run by the Department of State. Intended to help nations abroad set legal, regulatory and fiscal frameworks that will both ensure safe development and encourage foreign investment, UGTEP connects foreign countries with multiple U.S. Government agencies that work in tandem to share the U.S. experience and lessons learned. Both the industry and the host government will benefit from strong legal, regulatory and fiscal frameworks that will protect investments and the environment.

Question 2. What can the US do now to help our friends in Ukraine develop their own energy resources?

Answer. Today, the U.S. can continue to engage Ukraine on a bilateral basis to encourage the prudent development of its domestic resources, but the prospects for short-term success are limited so long as there is a high risk of civil war or Russian intervention in Ukraine. Such security challenges and political uncertainty raise the risks for any company interested in investing in Ukraine, and it is important that the resolution of those security concerns is the first priority.

In the long run, it is likely that U.S. companies will remain interested in the prospect of developing Ukraine's energy resources. The U.S. government can work with the new Ukrainian government to ensure that the legal and fiscal frameworks that it puts in place respect and protect foreign investments, providing a measure of certainty to companies interested in investing.

Question 3. Also please outline what kind of investment from the U.S. you believe would make a significant impact in Ukraine?

Answer. U.S. investment in energy efficiency technologies, offshore and unconventional gas, and energy transportation services would be helpful to Ukraine. All of these technologies would help to reduce Ukrainian dependence on gas imported from Russia, either by reducing the gas demand (through energy efficiency), or by reducing the need for Russian imports by increasing domestic production or creating new connections to European gas infrastructure.

Question 4. Can you discuss what role the North American energy alliance of the United States, Mexico, and Canada, can play in helping not only Ukraine but the rest of our allies around the world?

Answer. North America is growing increasingly more self-sufficient in energy production, a trend that has huge implications for our allies around the globe. While I focused on the growth of oil and gas production in the U.S. in my testimony, Canada has also seen its domestic production grow significantly and Mexico is currently undertaking major energy reforms that may change the outlook for their production as well. The benefits of increased self-sufficiency for North America are numerous: increased energy security, limited exposure to global price fluctuations, and even climate benefits from the production of natural gas. Our allies will also benefit, and in fact already have- Europe benefitted from the availability of LNG cargoes that were no longer needed by U.S. consumers after the beginning of the shale gas boom. The availability of North American energy on international markets will give our allies, many of who are dependent on imported energy, greater power when it comes to negotiating contracts for imports. The U.S. is considering energy exports today, and so is Canada. Like the U.S., Canada is viewed as a reliable global trading partner, and the availability of its energy resources on the global market would have a similar effect as exports of U.S. oil and gas. Our allies will benefit from reliable, competitively priced supplies of oil and gas, as well as from increased negotiating power.

Question 5. I believe that a strong case has been made for the U.S. to have a measurable impact on the global LNG market. We must allow export terminals to enter the market quickly enough to seize a piece of the growing global demand for LNG. It would seem, then, accelerated approval for those projects most likely to be built would have the greatest positive impact on our allies and our most reliable trade partners- what is your opinion on:

5a. Separating those projects that have spent considerable time and money to file with FERC into a separate approval queue?

5b. Separating those projects under the jurisdiction of United States Maritime Administration (MARAD), which currently has jurisdiction over two projects, into a separate queue in order to better reflect their different approval process and timeline?

Answer. Accelerating approval of commercially mature projects would provide an additional measure of certainty to the companies seeking to develop those projects, as well as to the foreign consumers that seek to contracts supplies of U.S. LNG. The

73

Department of Energy has been diligently completing the national interest determinations it is statutorily required to complete, and there have been few complaints about the agencies ability to successfully complete that process. Unfortunately, the chronological queue set by the Department does not take issues of commercial maturity into consideration. As such, mature projects that have spent considerably more time and money to attain their FERC approval may be forced to wait for DOE approval, in line behind projects that may not have even filed with FERC yet. I believe that there are ways to improve this process and provide commercially mature projects with some level of certainty that they will receive their export permits in time to complete their financing obligations and sign contracts with consumers. One option would be for DOE to make it clear that it will consider the applications of projects that have completed the FERC process or the MARAD process in advance of projects that have not. I explained more about this idea, which I have referred to as 'jump the queue,' in a piece for the Brookings Institution last year. It is my understanding that such a policy would within the Department's jurisdiction, and could even fall within the requirements of the Natural Gas Act that the agency should complete its national interest determination within 90 days of a final decision by FERC or MARAD.

Question 6. During the hearing we discussed the need for America to become an energy super power and ensure our allies have the ability to secure contracts and access natural gas free from fear of price gouging from non-democratic and anti-free market nations.

6a. With the current situation in Ukraine much has been made about Russia's long term gas contracts in Europe. Can you go into further detail about how many contracts Russia has in place with what countries and when they are set to expire?

Answer. Russia has long-term contracts with German and other gas consumers. The details of these contracts are not easily available and some of those contracts may be the subject, at least in part, of the European Union's anti-trust case against Gazprom. Russia has already renegotiated some of its long-term contracts to reflect more competitive prices, but they will have little impetus to renegotiate more contracts in the absence of competition for the European market from the U.S. and other alternative suppliers.

RESPONSES OF DAVID L. GOLDWYN TO QUESTIONS FROM SENATOR MURKOWSKI

Question 1. Please briefly describe your involvement in the creation of State Department's unconventional gas technical engagement function.

Answer. While serving as Secretary Clinton's Special Envoy for International Energy Affairs, my team and I evolved bilateral shale gas initiatives with China and India into the Global Shale Gas Initiative. We invited over 23 countries to a two-day workshop and site visit in August 2010 to learn how to develop their shale resources safely and efficiently. We subsequently began bilateral engagement under this rubric with Poland, Jordan, Morocco and Ukraine.

Question 2. Is expediting LNG exports from the U.S. still warranted even if the State Department technical engagement program is enhanced?

Answer. Yes, I believe that expedited LNG exports from the U.S. would be warranted even in the light of enhanced State Department UGTEP activity. Both increased availability of U.S. LNG and increased production of indigenous European natural gas would serve to help diversify Europe's gas supplies and provide the continent with greater negotiating power vis-a-vis Russia and other major exporters of natural gas. Both of these are long-term strategies in that neither will immediately provide additional gas to European consumers, but both could still provide immediate relief in the form of price negotiating power because of the importance of expectations in price-setting. The expectation of future supplies of gas, be they indigenous production or U.S. LNG, will help to push down prices of gas today.

Question 3. Is expediting LNG exports from the U.S. still warranted even if structural reforms are needed in Ukraine?

Answer. Yes, I would argue that the expedition of LNG exports from the U.S. is warranted regardless of the need for structural reforms in Ukraine, or in other countries. Access to competitively priced LNG supplies will benefit the economies of our allies significantly, even before structural reforms are complete. Structural reforms will remain important in the long run, in order to ensure that European energy markets operate efficiently and accurately price valuable goods like natural gas, but these reforms will take time. Market reforms are particularly important in Ukraine, which has long had disputes with Russia over the pricing of natural gas. If the price at which natural gas is sold internally in Ukraine continues to not reflect the true international market price of that commodity, then the nation will have significant difficulty meeting the terms of contracts for natural gas with suppliers other than Russia as well. While expedited LNG exports from the U.S. will be beneficial regardless of the status of structural reform, because they will put downward pressure on prices, Ukraine and many of its European neighbors will be unable to take full advantage of those benefits until reforms are fully implemented.

RESPONSE OF DAVID L. GOLDWYN TO QUESTION FROM SENATOR BARRASSO

Question 1. In your testimony, you state that: "[e]xports of LNG to Asia would be in the U.S.'s economic and strategic interests." You go on to explain that: "Russia aspires to double its share of the global LNG trade by 2020 in large part by meeting large shares of Asian demand growth." You note that Russia is seeking closer relationships with Japan and China. Finally, you ask whether: "we would prefer for Asia to plan to rely on Russian gas or on U.S. LNG as it builds its strategic alliances."

a. Would you explain how U.S. LNG exports are one of the few direct tools we possess to limit Russian market share in Asia?

Answer. As you noted from my testimony, Russia is moving aggressively to increase its market share in Asia. Asian buyers, including U.S. allies, will make decisions to enter into supply contracts largely on the basis of commercial interests rather than geopolitical concerns. Geopolitical issues will be taken into account only to the extent that they affect the competitiveness and reliability of the supplier. With these issues in mind, it is clear that one of the few tools the U.S. can utilize to directly limit Russia's market share is to allow U.S. firms to offer LNG at competitive prices in a way that is responsive to the commercial interests and needs that are preeminent in the minds of Asian buyers.

b. Would you explain how U.S. LNG exports will ensure that any Russian gas that is exported to Asia is done so at competitive prices?

Answer. In recent years LNG supplies made surplus by the US shale gas boom created a spot market for LNG that put downward pressure on Russian prices, forcing Gazprom to renegotiate contracts with several Western and Central European customers. In that case, the shale gas boom freed up LNG cargoes initially destined for the U.S. to European customers. Henry Hub-linked U.S. LNG contracts, even after accounting for liquefaction, transportation, and regasification costs, could render similar impacts in Asia. Like other consumers, Asian buyers value competitive costs, reliability, and timeliness. Russia has a history of expensive oil-linked contract prices, and ongoing events in Ukraine may bring into question whether it is a reliable, competitive supplier. To gain market share in Asia and obviate buyer concerns, Russia will therefore have to offer customers incentives—including concessions on price—if it is forced to compete with U.S. suppliers.

c. How does ensuring that Russian gas is sold at competitive prices-whether in Asia or Europe-serve U.S. strategic interests?

Answer. Continued high oil and gas export revenues are crucial to Russia's economy. The U.S. Energy Information Administration (EIA) estimates they account for over 50 percent of total Russian federal budget revenues. Declining oil and gas revenues may force Russia to diversify its economy and gradually embrace a model of broader, market-based economic growth, where new industries emerge whose leaders are less dependent on the largesse and goodwill from the authorities in Moscow. Lowering natural gas prices for allies in Asia and Europe helps their balance of trade, promotes growth in important export markets for the U.S. strengthens the economies of struggling allies, and makes natural gas more cost competitive versus coal, which advances US climate goals.

RESPONSES OF ADAM SIEMINSKI TO QUESTIONS FROM SENATOR LANDRIEU

Question 1. What are the prospects for increased production in the Haynesville shale? As you know, rig counts have been going down for some time, but your testimony seems to indicate it could be due for a comeback. What is driving this resurgence and could increasing exports expand it further? And why?

Answer. The number of drilling rigs in the Haynesville has risen from 45 in late 2013 to 54 as of March 2014. Recent increases in drilling activity and the high productivity of the wells currently being drilled has stemmed the decline in natural gas production from the Haynesville, which peaked at 10.5 billion cubic feet per day (Bcf/d) in November 2011 and has now stabilized around 6.5 Bcf/d in the first quarter of 2014. Natural gas production in the Haynesville is expected to increase in the coming months.

The Haynesville is currently an attractive and resurgent play for four reasons.

- Higher prices: With Henry Hub natural gas futures prices above $4.00, producers see an opportunity to drill profitable wells even outside of the most productive acreage.
- Below-average natural gas storage levels: After a very cold winter, working natural gas inventory is below normal levels going into the April through October injection season. Increased natural gas storage demand is supporting higher prices, and producers in the Haynesville may deploy more rigs to meet this demand.
- Pipeline capacity: With ample pipeline capacity to bring natural gas to nearby markets, producers do not experience long delays to tie new wells into takeaway infrastructure, as can be the case with new wells in the Marcellus.
- Proximity to proposed LNG export facilities: The Haynesville shale play is located in relative close proximity to the Sabine Pass LNG export terminal project, of which the first 1.1 Bcf/d of capacity is expected start operations during the fourth quarter of 2015, with another 1.1 Bcf/d of export capacity from that facility expected to become operational within the following two years. There are other proposed LNG export facilities in the Gulf region, which, if built, would also support demand for natural gas from the Haynesville.

Question 2. Concerns around exports have often been based on concerns around long term U.S. supply. Since you have been Administrator, estimates of U.S. gas supply have consistently gone in only one direction-up.

2a. Is EIA confident in the long term stability of natural gas supply?

2b. How have recent advances in technology and other factors contributed to this?

Answer. The U.S. has a relatively abundant supply of dry natural gas with technically recoverable resources at over 2,200 trillion cubic feet (Tcf) as of January 1, 2012. The growth in domestic natural gas production is supported primarily by increases in shale and tight gas investment and development, which is, in turn, supported by continual improvements in technology. Continued investment in the development of shale and tight gas is expected given the healthy demand growth for natural gas. In addition, further technological improvement and the continued application of 'best practices' in current developing plays will contribute to the economic viability of domestic natural gas supply. However, growth potential and sustainability of domestic production hinge around uncertainties in key assumptions, such as well production decline, lifespan, drainage areas, geologic extent, and technological improvement-both in areas currently being drilled and in those yet to be drilled. EIA reviews well-level production performances on a regular, on-going, basis and revises assumptions accordingly. The Low Oil and Gas Resource and High Oil and Gas Resource cases in the AEO2014 explore the effects of changes in Reference case assumptions about resource size and quality and technology advances. In all three cases, domestic natural gas production is projected to increase from the 2013 level of 24 Tcf. In the Reference case and the High Resource case, total natural gas production grows to 38 Tcf and 46 Tcf per year in 2040, respectively. In the Low Resource case, total natural gas production plateaus at just under 29 Tcf per year from 2027 through 2036, then declines to 28 Tcf in 2040.

An article in the Issues in focus section, "U.S. tight oil production: Alternative supply projections and an overview of EIA's analysis of well-level data aggregated to the county level," provides more information on the alternative resource cases.

RESPONSES OF ADAM SIEMINSKI TO QUESTIONS FROM SENATOR MURKOWSKI

Question 1. Has the Energy Information Administration noticed any supply disruptions or price dislocations resulting from increased natural gas exports via pipeline to Mexico and Canada in recent years?

Answer. EIA has not noticed any supply disruptions or price dislocations resulting from increased natural gas exports via pipeline to Mexico and Canada in recent years. U.S. natural gas exports via pipeline have grown 46% between 2010 and 2013.

U.S. natural gas pipeline exports to Canada accounted for 58% of total U.S. pipeline exports in 2013. The 911 billion cubic feet (Bcf) that was exported in 2013 is a 23% increase over 2010 export levels. Most U.S. natural gas exports to Canada occur at St. Clair, Michigan, which accounted for about 64% of total exports to Canada, although some of the gas exported at St. Clair originates in Canada. While exports have risen and imports have decreased in recent years, the United States was still a net importer from Canada in 2013.

In 2013, U.S. natural gas exports to Mexico were nearly double the level they were in 2010. In 2013, the U.S. exported a record 658 Bcf to Mexico. Exports to Mexico are largely used to supply electric power plants. As such, natural gas exports to Mexico show levels of seasonality counter to the majority of U.S. gas, peaking during the summer rather than winter months, when electric demand in Mexico is higher due to increased air conditioning load.

Question 2. The EIA forecasts certain levels of LNG exports from the U.S. in its reference case. Do you expect these export levels to have any impact on global LNG markets (e.g., on price, contract negotiations, etc.)?

Answer. EIA expects that introducing new lower priced supplies from the United States into the LNG market will place downward pressure on LNG prices and provide some additional leverage for buyers during contract negotiations, particularly in Asia. The degree that prices actually fall will also depend on additional supply, as well as demand, in the rest of the world. EIA is projecting U.S. LNG exports to reach 3.7 trillion cubic feet (Tcf) by 2030, with world LNG volumes at 20.6 Tcf. For perspective, in 2012, LNG supplied 12 Tcf or 10% of world consumption, imports via pipelines supplied 21%, and domestic production supplied the remaining.

While EIA has not studied the current or potential impact of U.S. LNG exports on contract negotiations, there is some anecdotal evidence and expert opinion that having potential U.S. LNG exporters negotiating with potential buyers around the world is influencing other contract negotiations, even before the United States has started to export LNG.

Question 3. Does the Department of Energy's Office of Fossil Energy have access to the latest EIA data and analysis pertaining to U.S. natural gas production and consumption, and forecasts of both?

Answer. All of EIA's data and analyses pertaining to U.S. natural gas production and consumption, and forecasts of both, are published on EIA's website. Staff within EIA and the Office of Fossil Energy have productive working relationships and regularly interact on both data and analysis issues, but there are no special access arrangements.

RESPONSE OF ADAM SIEMINSKI TO QUESTION FROM SENATOR CANTWELL

Question 1. During the hearing, there was much discussion of the analysis and forecasting of the effects of different levels of liquefied natural gas exports. I note that considerable government resources have been spent, and will continue to be spent, to ensure that our natural gas export policy remains in the public interest.

I am concerned that no such analysis yet exists to consider the effects of a potential reversal of the long-standing ban on crude oil exports. On February 3rd (over seven weeks ago), then-Chairman Wyden and I requested that your Administration look into potential market impacts of such a major policy change. While I understand that this kind of analysis requires considerable time and attention, I am concerned that it is not yet clear what kind of analysis EIA plans to undertake on this issue.

Our constituents would feel the impacts of any market changes that would be associated with such a major policy change, both in terms of prices that they would pay at the pump and the increased quantities of oil that would be finding new export transit routes, potentially via rail through Washington State.

How can we assure our constituents that their federal government will consider this issue thoroughly and thoughtfully?

Answer. The potential reversal of the long-standing ban on crude oil exports is one of a number of issues related to the implications of the dramatic rise in domestic oil production that the Energy Information Administration (EIA) is considering and about which EIA has already published information (see list that follows). EIA is continuing to analyze and address these issues and implications and intends to publish a series of focused analyses that will address effects of a possible relaxation of current limitations on U.S. oil exports as well as the following topics and issues related to the implications of the dramatic rise in domestic crude oil production:

- growth in U.S. oil production and trends in liquid fuels consumption
- impacts on oil logistics and refining
- crude oil and petroleum product prices
- crude oil and petroleum product trade patterns

Because of the dynamic nature of the U.S. crude oil and petroleum products markets, EIA intends to publish its findings in stages over the course of 2014. This will ensure that the most up-to-date data is incorporated in its work.

Short Term Energy Outlook

3/11/2014 STEO: EIA expects net import share to decline to 25% in 2015, lowest level since 1971

Annual Energy Outlook

12/16/2014 Slide 10: U.S. maintains status as a net exporter of petroleum products

Today In Energy

3/24/2014 China is now the world's largest net importer of petroleum and other liquid fuels

2/25/2014 Oil net imports have declined since 2011, with their value falling slower than volume

1/30/2014 Americas are an important market for liquid fuels and natural gas trade

1/22/2014 Oil and natural gas import reliance of major economies projected to change rapidly

1/9/2014 U.S. crude oil production growth contributes to global oil price stability in 2013

10/4/2013 U.S. expected to be largest producer of petroleum and natural gas hydrocarbons in 2013

This Week in Petroleum

3/12/2014 U.S. crude oil production in 2013 reaches highest level since 1989

1/23/2014 Crude oil imports continue to decline

1/8/2014 Strong U.S. crude oil production growth forecast through 2015

1/3/2014 Shifting production, demand patterns alter oil markets in 2013

10/30/2013 Recent decline in Gulf Coast crude oil imports mainly affects lighter grades

9/18/2013 Rail is Likely Supplying an Increasing Share of East Coast Crude Oil

8/14/2013 New Traffic Patterns Emerge to Supply Crude Oil to West Coast Refiners

7/10/2013 U.S. crude oil increasingly moves by barge, truck and rail

5/30/2013 Eastern Canadian refineries are increasing their use of U.S.-sourced crude oil

5/1/2013 Absorbing Increases in U.S. Crude Oil Production

4/3/2013 Mid-Continent Crude Oil Markets Continue to Adjust to Rapid Rise in Bakken Production

3/20/2013 Total U.S. crude oil imports continue to decline in 2012 but regional differences persist

1/16/2013 Upcoming Pipeline Capacity Additions Will Facilitate Continued Growth in Crude Oil Shipments from Midwest to Gulf Coast

1/9/2013 Strong U.S. Crude Oil Production Growth Forecast Through 2014

11/28/2012 Market Implications of Increased Domestic Production of Light Sweet Crude Oil

10/26/2012 The Impact of U.S. Crude Oil Production on Gulf Coast Crude Imports

Additional Material Submitted for the Record

STATEMENT OF ANITA ORBÁN, MINISTRY OF FOREIGN AFFAIRS, HUNGARY BEFORE THE HOUSE SUBCOMMITTEE ON ENERGY AND POWER OF THE ENERGY & COMMERCE COMMITTEE OF THE UNITED STATES HOUSE OF REPRESENTATIVES GEOPOLITICAL IMPLICATIONS OF LNG EXPORT LIBERALIZATION MARCH 25, 2014

Thank you Chairman Whitfield, Ranking Member Rush, and Members of the subcommittee. I appreciate the opportunity to be here today to provide my perspective on the importance of LNG export liberalization for the Central Eastern European region. I applaud the leadership of this Committee to look at the geostrategic aspect of US natural gas exports, which along with my colleagues from the Visegrad Group (currently chaired by Hungary), the Baltics and Eastern Europe we have been long advocating.

Mr. Chairman, we are in the middle of the largest security crisis that Europe has seen since the end of the Cold War. And energy dependence, especially that of Central Eastern Europe and Ukraine, is once again on everybody's mind. With every new Russo-Ukrainian crisis, US awareness about the strategic vulnerability of our region, and the determination to mitigate it, should only grow. Energy import dependence is one of the key factors that limit the political options available to these countries as US allies and adherents of a rules-based international order. Russian ambitions in the former post-Communist space are very clear and energy security is at the heart of this.

The European Union's dependence on external energy sources is massive. Today, Europe covers over 64 percent of its natural gas demand from imports. Approximately four-tenth of this import, i.e. 28 percent of Europe's total gas consumption, comes from Russia via three different routes—the Brotherhood pipeline via Ukraine, the Yamal pipeline via Belarus and the North Stream pipeline under the Baltic Sea. Sixty-two percent of Russia's natural gas exports to the EU go through the first route, i.e. via Ukraine.

The import dependence of EU member states varies widely, in the most extreme cases reaching 100 percent of their total gas consumption (Baltic States, Slovakia). But there is no country on the eastern side of the EU where the share of Russian gas imports is lower than 70 percent of its total gas import. One can contrast these figures with the situation in the United States, which in 2007, before the onset of the shale gas revolution, imported only 16 percent of its natural gas needs and U.S. unconventional gas explorations could make America the largest natural gas exporter by 2015.

The popular interpretation of energy dependence, and natural gas dependence, in particular, is widely associated with supply cut-offs which wouldn't be without precedent in Central Europe. Supply cut may indeed happen again with unpredictable consequences for countries along the Eastern border of the European Union, as well as for Ukraine. Yet, if used, it would seriously hurt the supplier as well: in the short term with loss of revenue, in the mid-term with loss of its markets. Supply cut-offs are so dramatic and so obviously political that they invariably trigger actions on the receiving end to ease the dependency. Moreover, one cannot cut off the supply for one country only—everybody along the pipeline route will suffer. A supply cut-off mobilizes and unites the dependent parties and results in decreasing dependency in the medium term. It is an absolute last-resort measure that ultimately undermines the very dependence that enabled it in the first place.

The best example to illustrate this point is the natural gas crisis of 2009. Then, Russia wanted to teach a lesson to Ukraine and cut off the gas going into the country. With it, Moscow discontinued the supply to most of Central Eastern Europe, as well. The crisis itself lasted for less than two weeks, but its most important impact was the ensuing cooperation and diversification efforts among the affected countries. A new approach emerged, whereby these countries connected their pipelines' North-South direction and enhanced their storage capacities, ultimately making each of them more crisis-resistant. Even more importantly, energy security came to the forefront of security considerations and became a flagship topic within the European Union. The Hungarian Visegrad Presidency also put this on top of the group's agenda for 2013-2014. Looking back, it would be hard to deny that the 2009 supply cut off was the single most important trigger event for improving the Central Eastern European region's energy security.

It is prices that provide the best economic and political tool for the monopoly supplier. Whoever has the monopoly, calls the shots: higher prices afflict a very tangible cost on the dependent country's economy and population, while stuffing the supplier's coffers and allowing it to reap the economic rents to finance further political, economic or military actions. Hiking prices can always be presented as pure business action as opposed to a foreign policy measure. Most importantly, it can be applied in a discriminatory manner. The supplier can raise the price for the non-cooperative and lower it for the friendly. Price movements, especially price discrimination, lead to asymmetrical negotiations and side-deals as opposed to transparency and, ultimately an affordable and secure energy supply for Europe.

The example of Ukraine is the most telling of all. The country currently imports about 26 billion cubic meters, or half of its consumption, of natural gas. All of its imports 4 come from Russia. Consequently, Moscow has been free to use price discrimination as it saw fit. Although the cost of gas grows linearly with the distance it travels, Germany pays less for the same Russian gas than any country on the route between the two. In fact, Russian gas in Germany was so much cheaper than the price paid by Ukraine that traders resold 2 billion cubic meters of this Russian-German gas to Ukraine in 2013.

In December 2013, Russia rewarded the former leaders of Ukraine with a 33 percent discount in natural gas prices for not signing the Association Agreement with the European Union. The new price of 268.5 dollars per thousand cubic meters is about 30 percent lower than the lowest price in the EU. As recent events in Ukraine have gone against the interests of Russia, Moscow is now raising the price to 400 dollars. Such a price would exact a massive toll on the already heavily indebted Ukrainian state. The only way to limit the monopoly supplier's ability to exact damage and sow discord through the deployment of the price weapon is to establish alternative supply routes. Once they are in place, the monopoly supplier can no longer use the price discrimination tool freely, as it needs to consider how its actions affect the viability and attractiveness of alternative supply channels.

The recent deal between Gazprom and the Greek gas company DEPA is a case in point. In February this year, Gazprom agreed to a 15 percent price cut for Greece to be applied retroactively for about 7 months. Experts claim that Greece's LNG terminal and the recent developments in the Southern Gas Corridor, which will bring Azeri gas to Greece, among other countries, in the medium term factored into the negotiations. Simply put, the mere existence of a credible alternative supplier exerted significant downward pressure on the natural gas prices set by the dominant supplier.

We are well aware of the fact that alternative pipeline gas won't reach Europe before 2019 the earliest. Azeri gas coming in via the Southern Gas Corridor will benefit Western Europe via Italy rather than Central and South Eastern Europe. Consequently, for Central Eastern European countries, the most important task is to create a credible prospect for alternative natural gas imports.

To do that, Central Eastern Europe needs to ensure both the capacity and the volume to receive alternative gas. The first is our homework, which only we can do to build up capacities internally which allow gas-to-gas competition, create access to different supply options and create a robust internal European energy infrastructure. In Central Eastern Europe we need to overcome the dependency inherent in the traditional East-West pipeline infrastructure in the former Soviet satellite states by constructing North-South and South-North interconnectors with the aim to have a robust North-South and South-North pipeline infrastructure from the Agean to the Baltic Sea. Another important aspect is enabling the reverse flow of natural gas on these newly built, as well as older interconnections especially from the West to the East to ensure that regional markets become truly integrated.

However, Europe has been much less successful in building up the necessary volumes for alternative supply. This has been largely out of Europe's control. EU and US sanctions against Iran, the slower than expected progress in Iraq, the upheaval in North Africa postponed or put on hold indefinitely most of the potential alternative pipeline supplies. The only new supply volumes coming in from Azerbaijan as of 2019 are exactly the same quantity as the total supply from Libya which stopped entirely at the end of 2013, an annual 10 billion cubic meters.

What Central Eastern Europe and the EU in general needs right now is the additional volume of gas. The most viable option Central Eastern Europeans have today is LNG. The LNG market has numerous advantages: many suppliers, liquidity and prices set by supply and demand with no political strings attached. Access to the LNG market would much weaken the dependence inherently present in pipeline deliveries.

Access to LNG would also assist Ukraine. During 2013, two additional capacities were opened from Hungary to Ukraine and from Poland to Ukraine, enabling the supply of natural gas to Ukraine on purely market terms. If successful, the LNG supply together with the existing and planned additional reverse flow capabilities, combined with Ukraine's own shale gas resources, could provide a reasonably sized alternative to Russian gas in Ukraine.

However, in the absence of an energy security contribution from US exports, the global supply of LNG is not at all reassuring. Among LNG exporters, terrorist and insurgent activity impacts gas operations in Yemen, Libya, Egypt, Nigeria and Algeria. Qatar has a moratorium on further exports, while in Asia, some important traditional exporters like Indonesia are now in decline. To the extent supply grows, it is locked into rigid long term contracts that can't provide flexible resilience. Without the large shale gas resources and efficient competitive markets of the United States, LNG cannot provide an adequate energy security answer.

The urgency of establishing the region's access to LNG means that the United States Congress has a potent foreign policy/energy diplomacy tool at its disposal. By clearing the way for US shale gas to reach America's Central European NATO allies would provide significant protection against the deployment of the energy/price weapon.

Today, natural gas prices in the United States are one-third to one-fourth of the gas prices in Europe, including in Central Europe. Liberalizing US LNG exports would send a signal to market actors to kick-start the development of missing infrastructure (LNG terminals, interconnectors). These developments in turn would put an immediate downward pressure on gas prices in Central Eastern Europe well before a single American gas molecule reaches the shores of our region. Energy diplomacy is not about short term fixes, we operate with long-term investments and decades long contracts, we know that the timeframe for US gas exports is 3-7 years.

But it is simply not true that lifting the natural gas export ban today would not have an immediate effect in the region. It would immediately change the business calculus of infrastructure investments and send an extremely important message of strategic reassurance to the region which currently feels more threatened than any time since the Cold War. Even with regasification, shipping and associated costs, US gas would be regarded as an important alternative. And let's not forget that countries in our region are ready to pay a premium price for energy security.

In short, by liberalizing LNG exports, by eliminating the legal and administrative obstacles to the free trading of this vital, domestically produced commodity, the United States would provide fast and long-lasting protection for its allies against the most important dangers of natural gas dependency. Moreover, it would also enable them to act more freely in assisting Ukraine in case of an energy crisis developed there. Such a help would be in line with past US leadership in Central Eastern Europe, which many in our region have perceived to be waning in the past few years. It is important to note that this is an elegant, yet very effective tool, which is relatively cheap to use. It incurs no threat of loss of life, not even a disruption of economic activities: it is only a removal of a self-imposed barrier. Moreover, it cannot be seen as targeting any single entity- it is only a form of help for allies, a common sense solution that helps allies and US businesses at home. It would be hard to find any other tool so obviously at hand to the US to demonstrate leadership right now, have an immediate security impact at a relatively low cost.

Hungary, as chair of the Visegrad group (Poland, Czech Republic, Slovakia, Hungary) together with several other US allies argued for LNG export liberalization even before the Ukraine crisis started. We have reached out to members of Congress and the administration to argue that the US has a historic opportunity to send a strong message of freedom to the region by simply letting the markets work. Together with my Czech colleague, Vaclav Bartuska, we have argued that "accelerating the export licensing procedure to allow increased sales to trustworthy, reliable foreign partners should be a policy that politicians on both sides of the aisle can support." This is not a partisan issue. It is an American issue that all statesmen in this country must show leadership on. Numerous Members of Congress recognized the geopolitical importance of LNG export by introducing and co-sponsoring the different bills that proposed to lift the ban on export licensing. The situation in Ukraine only underlines how timely this issue is—but also gives it additional urgency. The US should seize the opportunity and act now.

Mr. Chairman, Members of the Committee, I believe that doing away with these export limitations would make economic sense even in better times. But there is nothing like a crisis to focus the mind. As representatives of a country that Central Europe has traditionally looked to for leadership, you know well that you do not always have the luxury of choosing the time to make some of the most necessary decisions. But with the post-Cold War settlement crumbling before our eyes, if there was ever a time for your leadership, it is now—and if there was ever an issue that would do as much good at as little cost, it is the issue at hand.

———

STATEMENT OF THE AMERICAN PUBLIC GAS ASSOCIATION

A CONSUMER PERSPECTIVE

On behalf of the American Public Gas Association (APGA), thank you for the opportunity to submit testimony for the hearing titled, "Importing Energy, Exporting Jobs. Can it be Reversed?"

APGA is the national association for publicly owned natural gas distribution systems. There are approximately 1,000 public gas systems in 36 states and over 700 of these systems are APGA members. Publicly owned gas systems are not-for-profit, retail distribution entities owned by, and accountable to, the citizens they serve. They include municipal gas distribution systems, public utility districts, county districts, and other public agencies that own and operate natural gas distribution facilities in their communities. Public gas systems' primary focus is on providing safe, reliable, and affordable service to their customers. The long-term affordability of natural gas has been a focus of APGA and its members.

APGA has the privilege of representing the views of American natural gas consumers. We represent the homeowners and small businesses that rely on affordable natural gas to heat their homes, cook their meals, power their restaurants, operate small manufacturing entities, and service businesses. The interests of these millions of Americans have often been lost in the contentious debate about liquefied natural gas (LNG) exports. Media outlets have framed the debate as oil and gas companies on one side and manufacturers on the other.[1]

However, as advocates for natural gas consumers, our position is slightly different from the manufacturing companies that have spoken out on the issue. Simply put, APGA opposes all exports of LNG from the lower 48 states. The simple economics of supply and demand, along with every study that has been conducted on the subject, whether done by the federal government or by private consulting companies, all reach one conclusion: exports will increase the price of domestic natural gas. How adverse that upward pressure on price will be, no one knows. Based on past experience though, APGA believes the experts who supported the export of propane would not have predicted the significant adverse prices homeowners paid this winter for their propane.

What this means for average consumers is that their energy bill for natural gas service, electricity, and the goods and services they purchase—all of which have the cost of energy built into their prices—will escalate. We can debate about net benefits, aggregate welfare measures, and other economic metrics, but ultimately LNG export translates into people paying more for energy and other goods and services, and consequently having less disposable income. This fact applies to businesses as well. As energy costs go up, companies are less competitive and hire fewer workers, whether they serve customers down the street or compete for customers around the globe.

Before discussing the details of APGA's opposition to the export of LNG, there is one message that we would like Congress to focus on when thinking about this issue: it is irrefutable that consumers and businesses will pay increased prices for energy and all goods and services if LNG exports are sanctioned.

LNG Export

The Department of Energy Office of Fossil Energy (DO- FE) commissioned two studies regarding the effects of LNG exports. The first, conducted by the U.S. Energy Information Administration (EIA), studied the impact of LNG exports on domestic prices and concluded that exports will increase prices with higher volumes causing more drastic increases.[2] The second, conducted by NERA Economic Con-

———

[1] PGA is a proud member of America's Energy Advantage (AEA), which represents the interests of bothmanufacturers and natural gas consumers.

[2] Effect of Increased Natural Gas Exports on Domestic Energy Markets, U.S. Energy Information Administration (Jan. 2012) ("EIA Export Report"). As requested by the DOE/FE, the EIA Export Report considered four scenarios: (1) 6 Bcf/d phased in at a rate of 1 Bcf/d per year (low/

sulting, focused on the macroeconomic effects of LNG exports, which were found to be a net positive while at the same time confirming that LNG exports would raise domestic natural gas prices. This would ultimately burden the U.S. consumers who can least afford the increase and disadvantage domestic manufacturing.[3] Policy-makers must consider both of these studies-and and other non-governmental studies on the subject-and in doing so, consider the profound tradeoffs entailed by exporting away an increasingly valuable U.S. fuel resource rather than supporting its use domestically.

Increased production of natural gas in the U.S. to meet domestic demand provides the nation with an unprecedented opportunity to pursue energy independence and sustained economic growth through a manufacturing renaissance grounded in plentiful, low cost natural gas. Price increases will also jeopardize the viability of natural gas as a bridge fuel in the transition away from carbon-intensive and otherwise environmentally problematic coal-fired electric generation and inhibit efforts to foster natural gas as a major transportation fuel, which is important in weaning the U.S. from its historic and high-risk dependence on foreign oil.

Background

To date, over 30 applications have been submitted to DOE to export domestic LNG from the United States to free trade agreement (FTA) or non-FTA nations based on the promise of huge unconventional domestic gas reserves and huge profits for the few affected companies. Of those applications, six have already been approved, meaning that 8.5 Bcf/day has been approved by DOE for export to non-FTA countries. Also to date, the total export capacity applied for is 38.51Bcf/d and 35.86 Bcf/d to FTA and non-FTA nations, respectively. Total natural gas production was approximately 67 Bcf/d in the U.S. in 2013[4]; therefore, based on current data, the total applied-for export capacity, if authorized, would have the potential effect of increasing the demand for natural gas by nearly 54 percent.

Policymakers in Congress and at DOE have a duty to ensure that any non-FTA application under consideration for export authority is not inconsistent with the public interest pursuant to NGA section 3(a).[5] The "public interest analysis of export applications" should be "focused on domestic need for natural gas," threats to domestic supply, and "other factors to the extent they are shown to be relevant."[6]

For exports of LNG to countries with which the United States has a free trade agreement, the application for export authority is automatically assumed to be in the public interest and is granted almost instantly without opportunity for the public to comment.

For exports to non-FTA countries, which are the focal point for the current export debate, DOE adopts a rebuttable presumption that exports are in the public interest. Those opposed to exports face a nearly insurmountable challenge of proving a negative; more specifically, that each individual application is not in the public interest. APGA has filed motions to intervene and protests every non-FTA application, pointing out the deleterious impacts of the applications on the nation's consumers and businesses, relying on, among other materials, the EIA Export Report and the NERA Study. But since APGA does not have the resources to conduct independent detailed market impact analyses for each application in order to prove to DOE that exports are not in the public interest, the die is cast and the export applications are granted.

APGA believes that the burden of proof should be shifted to exporting companies. Companies that seek to export the U.S.'s plentiful—but ultimately finite-reserves of a strategic commodity should have to prove to DOE that exporting LNG benefits not merely their bottom line, nor oil and gas producers, but all sectors of the economy including natural gas consumers. Surely, consideration of the public interest requires no less.

---

slow scenario); (2) 6 Bcf/d phased in at a rate of 3 Bcf/d per year (low/rapid scenario); (3) 12 Bcf/d phased in at a rate of 1 Bcf/d per year (high/slow scenario); and (4) 12 Bcf/d phased in at a rate of 3 Bcf/d per year (high/rapid scenario).

[3] Macroeconomic Impacts of LNG Exports from the United States, NERA Economic Consulting (Dec. 2012) ("NERA Study"). APGA understands (and applauds the fact) that the merits and demerits of the NERA Study will be assessed independently by DOE/FE in a separate proceeding (77 Fed. Reg. 73627); and hence APGA's comments here on the NERA Study are only preliminary and not intended to represent its complete assessment of the NERA Study.

[4] See: http://www.eia.gov/naturalgas/issuesandtrends/production/2013/

[5] 15 U.S.C. § 717b(a).

[6] Sabine Pass Liquefaction, LLC, Opinion and Order Denying Request for Review Under Section 3(c) of the Natural Gas Act, October 21, 2010, FE Docket No. 10-111-LNG.

LNG Exports Will Increase Domestic Natural Gas Prices

According to the EIA Export Report, "[l]arger export levels lead to larger domestic price increases."[7] EIA also concluded that "rapid increases in export levels lead to large initial price increases," but that slower increases in export levels will "eventually produce higher average prices during the decade between 2025 and 2035."[8]

Even under the "low/slow" baseline scenario in the EIA Export Report, price impacts will reach about 14 percent.[9] Under the "low/rapid" baseline scenario, EIA projects that wellhead prices will be approximately 18 percent higher in 2016 than they otherwise would be.[10] In fact, under all of the low scenarios accounting for different economic and shale reserve conditions, EIA predicts price impacts well above 10 percent that then moderate.[11] Under the "high/rapid" scenario, EIA projects that prices will increase by 36 percent to 54 percent by 2018 depending on natural gas supplies and economic growth. It is important to note that the low/slow baseline assumed an export level of 6 Bcf/day, which as noted above has already been exceeded in terms of approvals, and that the high/rapid scenario assumed an export level of 12 Bcf/day, which appears imminent given recent actions by DOE.

The NERA study also concluded that the higher the volume of LNG exports, the more domestic natural gas prices will rise. Both studies underestimate potential price increases because they are based on outdated projections of domestic demand for natural gas and the questionable assumption that the demand for natural gas is sufficiently elastic to prevent significant price spikes.

Domestic Demand Underestimated

On December 16, 2013, the EIA issued the Early Release of its Annual Energy Outlook for 2014 (AEO2014). The AEO2014 projects greater increases in domestic demand for natural gas than projected in prior Annual Energy Outlooks. In particular, the AEO2014 projects greater increases in demand for natural gas from domestic industry, particularly from the bulk chemicals and metals-based durables shipments, which "grow by 3.4 percent per year from 2012-2025.as compared to 1.9 percent in AEO 2013."[12]

AEO2014 also projects greater increases in future reliance on natural gas for electric generation than projected by the EIA in previous Annual Energy Outlooks. In fact, the AEO2014 Reference case projects that by 2040 natural gas will account, "for 35 percent of total electricity generation, while coal accounts for 32 percent."[13] In AEO2013, natural gas would only overtake coal in terms of the share of electric generation by 2040 under the High Oil and Gas Resource scenario and would not have done so under the Reference case.

Moreover, the shift to natural gas for electric generation will be further increased by the forthcoming implementation of the Environmental Protection Agency's (EPA) pending Mercury Air Toxic Standards (MATS), which will force the retirement of a large number of coal-fired generators.

Both studies commissioned by DOE-FE rely on projected natural gas demand from AEO2011. These outdated projections fail to account for current EIA expectations regarding future demand and tend to overestimate demand elasticity, or the ability of natural gas consumers to curtail their purchases in response to higher prices in the electric generation sector. Once a coal plant is retired due to MATS, or for any other reason, the operator of the retired plant cannot switch it back on in response to higher natural gas costs. Meanwhile, the EPA's new greenhouse gas standards for new electric generators virtually ensure that new coal plants will not be constructed to replace those that are retired.[14] Soon, electric generation companies will not only demand more gas but also rely on it more heavily for base load production, altering expectations about demand elasticity that prognosticators have relied on when assuming that natural gas prices will not rise sharply due to LNG exports.[15]

---

[7] Id. at 6.

[8] Id.

[9] Id. at 8.

[10] Id.

[11] Id. at 9.

[12] AEO2014 Early Release Overview at 1.

[13] AEO2014 Early Release at 2.

[14] "Standards of Performance for Greenhouse Gas Emissions for New Stationary Sources: Electric Utility Generating Units" 77 C.F.R. 22392 (Apr. 13, 2012).

[15] See Energy Information Administration, Fuel Competition in Power Generation and Elasticities of Substitution (June 2012) (general description of fuel switching and price elasticity among fuels in the power generation sector) available at http://www.eia.gov/analysis/studies/fuelelasticities/pdf/eia-fuelelasticities.pdf.

This same trend would also exacerbate the increases in the price of electricity caused by LNG exports that are projected by the EIA and NERA.

While demand elasticity will shrink in the electric sector, leading to sharper increases in natural gas and electricity prices than previously forecasted, manufacturers will continue to be responsive to increases in the price of natural gas-meaning that manufacturers will curtail consumption and hence production due to higher prices. Congress and the DOE need to examine what this means for the economy and the broader public interest of the nation in its consideration of this and other LNG export applications.

Effects of Higher Prices

Increases in the price of natural gas will impact the U.S. consumers who can least afford the price increase, inhibit the expansion of domestic manufacturing, and forestall the further use of natural gas as a bridge fuel away from carbon-intensive coal for generation and from foreign sourced oil for transportation. The NERA study demonstrates that the effects of LNG exports and the attendant price increases are tantamount to a "wealth transfer" from poor and middle class Americans to those with investments in the natural gas industry. The DOE-FE should examine what this wealth transfer would entail for the public interest when evaluating LNG export applications. Congress must do likewise in considering the state of LNG exports.

Hurts Economically Vulnerable Households

LNG exports will raise domestic natural gas prices, which will increase costs to households that rely on natural gas for heating and cooking. NERA projects that these higher costs will be offset by increases in the value of natural gas resources and related companies, which NERA assumes many Americans own through retirement savings and other investments.[16]

However, the validity of that assumption is highly questionable since according to a Pew Research survey, "53 percent of Americans say they have no money at all invested in the stock market, including retirement accounts."[17]

Furthermore, merely owning stock does not guarantee an individual will own stock in an oil and gas company or exporting company, without which an individual will not directly benefit from LNG exports. Taking the analysis a step further, even if an individual does own stock and owns oil and gas company/exporting company stock, the key question is, does that person own enough shares to offset the price increases for energy, goods, and services that will result from LNG exports. This distribution of stock ownership casts significant doubt that a majority of Americans own oil and gas/exporter stock in sufficient quantities to offset energy price increases.

NERA does admit, however, that "[h]ouseholds with income solely from wages or government transfers," will not share in the benefits of increased profits from natural gas.[18] Therefore, the increase in natural gas prices due to exports will impact most those consumers without investments or retirement savings, those living paycheck-to-paycheck or relying on government assistance, which includes the 46.5 million people that live in poverty in the U.S.[19] Even beyond Americans who live in poverty, the majority of Americans, some 167 million people, will only incur the costs of exports and none of the benefits.

Suppresses Other Domestic Industries

The NERA study indicates that as the price of natural gas increases, the economy demands or produces fewer goods and services. This results in lower wages and capital income for consumers; under such economic conditions, consumers save less of their income for investment.

As a result, industries that rely on natural gas will experience "a reduction in overall output," mitigated by a "switch to fuels that are relatively cheaper."[20] The latter argument assumes that alternatives to natural gas are affordable and available, which is an invalid assumption for fertilizer manufacturers and many other industries.

Moreover, the NERA study identified chemical manufacturing as one of the natural gas and energy intensive industries that will be among the most severely dis-

---

[16] See Markey Letter (casting doubt on the assumption that benefits to the natural gas sector will be widely enjoyed by ordinary American via retirement investments).
[17] See: http://www.pewresearch.org/fact-tank/2013/05/31/stocks-and-the-recovery-majority-of-americans- not-invested-in-the-market/
[18] NERA Study at 8.
[19] See: http://www.nclej.org/poverty-in-the-us.php
[20] NERA Study at 53.

advantaged due to natural gas price increases caused by LNG exports.[21] According to NERA "[d]omestic industries for which natural gas is a significant component of their cost structure will experience increases in their cost of production, which will adversely impact their competitive position in a global market and harm U.S. consumers who purchase their goods."[22] Leaders in the chemical sector have voiced concern regarding LNG exports and adverse impacts on the industry caused by inflated natural gas prices.[23]

When evaluating whether export applications are consistent with the public interest, policymakers must ask not only "what will we gain from LNG exports," but also "what will we give up." A U.S. manufacturing renaissance that promises greater economic growth and job creation with positive effects rippling throughout the economy hangs in the balance. Right now, industry is poised to invest billions of dollars in new natural gas intensive facilities in the U.S. premised on the promise of low domestic natural gas prices. For example, Sasol North America, Inc. is currently considering investing in the first gas to liquids plant in the U.S., an innovative technology for producing diesel and other liquid fuels without oil, and U.S. natural gas prices are a primary consideration regarding whether the investment will go forward.[24]

Affordable natural gas prices in the U.S. provide the path forward for the manufacturing renaissance. Higher natural gas prices due to LNG exports threaten this promising return to American manufacturing, and prior economic data demonstrate that when domestic energy prices increase, the country loses manufacturing jobs, particularly in the fertilizer, plastics, chemicals, and steel industries.[25]

Rather than trading long-term manufacturing jobs for short-term natural gas-related construction jobs, the DOE-FE should pursue policies that create new manufacturing jobs and broader economic growth in the U.S. Using natural gas for manufacturing provides a value-added benefit to the economy because industry multiplies the value of every dollar it expends on natural gas for energy or as a raw material. Rather than investing in natural gas exports, which squeeze out investments from other sectors of the economy, the U.S. should pursue policies that allow industry to invest in natural gas dependent manufacturing. Energy and natural gas intensive manufacturing produces chemicals, metals, cement and other materials that may be add low-value, but create positive ripple effects up the value chain and throughout the economy.[26] Rather than exporting natural gas as a raw natural resource, the U.S. could export processed materials, such as steel, or higher value-added goods at more competitive prices, with greater benefits to the U.S. job market and GDP.

Threaten Transition from Coal

Current low natural gas prices provide an opportunity to wean the U.S. off of carbon-intensive coal. Inflated natural gas prices due to LNG exports will decrease the viability of natural gas as a bridge fuel to a lower carbon future. Current low prices make natural gas-fired electricity generation an economically sound alternative to coal-fired generation. Sustained low prices may encourage this transition by private initiative regardless of increased environmental regulations as investors find natural gas competitive with coal. If exports inflate natural gas prices, the economics turn against cleaner burning natural gas.[27]

As discussed above, new greenhouse gas regulations will also soon force coal retirements. If natural gas prices remain low, the U.S. may be able to transition away from carbon intensive coal without causing electricity prices to increase significantly. If natural gas prices are high, however, electricity prices will spike as rel-

---

[21] NERA Study at 64.

[22] NERA Study at 13.

[23] Press Release, Dow Chemical, DOE Report on LNG Exports Short Changes Manufacturing and U.S. Competitiveness (Dec. 6, 2012) available at http://www.dow.com/news/press-releases/article/?id=6138

[24] Clifford Kraus, South African Company to Build U.S. Plant to Convert Gas to Liquids, New York Times (Dec. 3, 2012) available at: http://www.nytimes.com/2012/12/04/business/energy-environment/sasol-plans-first-gas-to-liquids-plant-in-us.html?___r=0.

[25] U.S. House Committee on Natural Resources Democrats, Drill Here, Sell There, Pay More: The Painful Price of Exporting Natural Gas (March 2012) available at http://democrats.naturalresources.house.gov/reports/drill-here-sell-there-pay-more.

[26] NERA claims that harm resulting from exports will "likely be confined to very narrow segments of industry," namely low value-added, energy intensive manufacturing. NERA Study at 67-69. NERA, however, ignores the benefits of producing materials in the U.S. that can then be used by other U.S. manufactures that are less energy intensive and higher up the value chain. For instance, if plastics are produced at competitive prices in the U.S., toy manufacturers may find it economical to "re-shore" toy manufacturing plants. Steven Mufson, The New Boom: Shale Gas Fueling an American Industrial Revival, Washington Post (Nov. 14, 2012).

[27] EIA Export Report at 17.

atively cheap coal-fired generators are forced to retire for regulatory reasons. Spiking electricity rates will have rippling effects on the U.S. economy, especially energy intensive, cost-sensitive manufacturing.

Keeps the U.S. Dependent on Foreign Oil

Currently, the U.S. imports billions of dollars of oil from around the globe, a great deal of which is used as gasoline to fuel vehicles. The replacement of current gasoline-powered fleets with natural gas vehicles would significantly reduce U.S. dependence on foreign oil, and thereby enhance U.S. security and strategic interests and reduce our trade deficit.[28] State governments, businesses and many of APGA's members are expending substantial resources today to put the needed infrastructure in place.[29]

Automobiles are not the only modes of transportation that businesses are interested in transitioning to natural gas. A company in Canada is investing in commercial locomotives powered by LNG and teaming up with Caterpillar to employ similar technology in heavy duty equipment that currently runs on diesel.[30] If Congress and the DOE allow export applications to go through, the resulting increase in natural gas prices could undermine recent investments to expand natural gas as a transportation fuel.

Policymakers should not pursue an export policy that undermines the efficient, domestic use of a domestic fuel stock and America's first and best opportunity to move toward energy independence by decreasing reliance on foreign oil.

U.S. and Foreign Natural Gas Prices Will Converge

Currently, there are significant disparities between domestic natural gas commodity prices and prices in some nations that rely on LNG imports. These disparities provide would-be exporters with appealing arbitrage opportunities in the short-term, but they will not last. Gas rich shale deposits are a global phenomenon, just now beginning to be tapped. Also, despite relatively low domestic natural gas prices, certain countries, such as Qatar, can produce massive quantities of natural gas at even lower prices. As other nations develop their resources and export capacity, and as U.S. natural gas prices increase due to export, international and domestic prices will converge, leaving the U.S. with higher domestic prices that thwart energy independence and that undermine the competitiveness of the manufacturing sector that relies heavily on natural gas as a process fuel.

The U.S. is at the forefront of technology in the development of shale gas reserves. A recent study by MIT concludes that the U.S. should export its technology and expertise.[31] According to MIT, the development of international unconventional natural gas reserves will create a more liquid market with less disparity between prices around the globe.[32]

The U.S. should follow this strategy, instead of spending billions of dollars to build facilities in order to export a commodity that will possibly be abundant worldwide before the LNG export facilities can even be completed.[33]

The U.S. has an opportunity that was unimaginable two or three years ago to significantly expand its manufacturing sector, transition away from our reliance on coal-fired electricity generation without risking price shocks, and finally make real progress towards energy independence. All of this, however, depends on relatively low and stable natural gas prices, which sharply contrasts with the history of nat-

---

[28] Cheniere and other exporters claim that their proposed exports will benefit the U.S. balance of trade, but it does not consider the benefits to the trade balance of cutting oil imports and exporting value-added goods manufactured in the U.S. with affordable natural gas.

[29] Officials are planning a series of compressed natural gas ("CNG") filling pumps at existing filling stations across the Pennsylvania US Route 6, stretching 400 miles from New York State near Milford, Pike County, Pa. in the east and through Crawford County, Pa. to the Ohio state line on the west, known as "PA Route 6 CNG Corridor;" at the same time, Chesapeake Energy is converting its vehicles in northeastern Pennsylvania to CNG and working with a local convenience-store chain and transit authority to foster further CNG integration. Eric Hrin, Pennsylvania Looks to CNG, The Daily Review Online (May 26, 2011) available at http://thedailyreview.com/news/pennsylvania-looks-to-cng-1.1135267; see also, Texas S.B. 20 (On July 15, 2011, the governor of Texas signed S.B. 20, supporting a network of natural gas-refueling stations along the Texas Triangle between Dallas/Ft. Worth, San Antonio, and Houston. The new legislation will lay a foundation for wider-scale deployment of heavy-duty, mid- and light-duty natural gas vehicles ("NGVs") in the Texas market).

[30] Rodney White, Firm on Track to Build LNG-Fueled Locomotive, Platts Gas Daily (Nov. 28, 2012).

[31] MIT Energy Initiative, The Future of Natural Gas, at 14 (2011).

[32] Id.

[33] The U.S. should be ever mindful of the billions of dollars invested in LNG import facilities, which are white elephants that stand as testaments to the extent to which technology at home or abroad can undermine investments that ignore the portability of technology.

ural gas price volatility. Congress and the DOE should not turn a blind eye and allow the same businesses that gambled and lost on projections of the need for future natural gas imports to now potentially squander our nation's future on what may well turn out to be another failed venture as natural gas production and export capacity develop throughout the world.

Alternative Approach

The United States should be exporting the drilling technology that has enabled producers in this country to tap into our huge shale reserves. There are likewise vast shale reserves in Europe, including in Ukraine, that are there for the taking, assuming the selfsame countries are willing to invest in the technology to access those reserves and also to permit drilling for shale gas reserves. There is certainly no good reason why the U.S should undertake a domestic LNG export policy that has numerous downsides for the American gas consumers when many of the very countries we are seeking to help are capable of helping themselves by accessing their own domestic shale gas reserves.

In lieu of exporting our affordable premium fossil fuel, Congress should focus on adopting policies that encourage greater domestic demand for natural gas and greater emphasis on exporting drilling technology to WTO and other countries that have the capability to access natural gas reserves. It is a much better choice, in both the short and long term, to accelerate the transition in the United States from imported oil to domestic natural gas to fuel our transportation sector, revitalize our manufacturing industry, and improve our balance of trade.

Conclusion

APGA appreciates the opportunity to submit testimony on this critical natural gas and public interest issue. We stand ready to work with the Committee on these and all other natural gas issues.

————

NORTH AMERICA'S BUILDING TRADES UNIONS,
March 26, 2014.

Hon. MARY LANDRIEU,
Chairwoman,

Hon. LISA MURKOWSKI,
Ranking Member, 304 Dirksen Senate Office Building, Washington, DC.

DEAR CHAIRWOMAN LANDRIEU & RANKING MEMBER MURKOWSKI;

On behalf of the three million skilled craft professionals in the United States and Canada comprising the fourteen national and international unions of the Building and Construction Trades Department, AFL-CIO, I am pleased the Senate Energy and Natural Resources Committee held the March 25, 2014, hearing entitled Importing Energy, Exporting Jobs. Can it be Reversed? Our members stand ready to be part of a solution. We believe a modern U.S. energy policy, encompassing enhanced energy security and a self-reliant North American production capacity, will result in economic prosperity and robust job creation.

During this shift from a net energy importer to one of the world's largest producers, a labor force comprised of skilled craftsmen and women will be necessary to construct the pipelines and build the facilities needed to support domestic production. The Building Trades can provide the skilled labor and craftsmanship needed to meet this looming construction boom. And our 100 years of experience with successful, sustainable, high quality joint labor-management apprenticeship programs (JATC) ensure the demand for skilled craft professionals will be met with the best-trained, most well-equipped workforce in the world.

JATCs collectively spend more than $1 billion in private funding annually on apprenticeship instructors, curriculum, and job placement. The unionized construction industry (labor and management acting together) also invest, through collective bargaining, an additional $11 billion annually on wages and benefits. To give some perspective to the size of our JATC training system, managing and operating roughly 1,900 training centers across North America, if it was a singular college or university, it would be the second largest in the US.

Our system of apprenticeship training and education has become world renowned for several reasons:

- We maintain a direct linkage to the labor market
- Our apprentices earn while they learn
- There is continuity of employment over the three to five year training program driven by labor-management commitment
- We integrate employment and training

In addition to our apprenticeship programs, we are extremely proud of our "Helmets to Hardhats" program. This non-profit organization connects National Guard, Reserve, retired and transitioning active-duty military service members with apprenticeship training and career opportunities in the construction industry. The program's Wounded Warrior initiative connects wounded veterans with non-field careers and accommodations in construction. During its ten-year existence, "Helmets to Hardhats" has placed thousands of veterans in jobs and career training opportunities.

Given our track record of training and supplying world-class craftsmen and women to work in the construction industry, North America's Building Trades members stand ready to serve as the foundation of this exciting energy revolution and construct the infrastructure needed to transform our domestic energy industry into the envy of the world.

We are thrilled your chairmanship coincides with this pivotal point in US energy policy. We stand ready to work with you and the committee in any capacity to ensure our energy policy drives job creation and economic prosperity.

Sincerely,

SEAN MCGARVEY,
President.

○